PURELY BELTER

Writer-director **MARK HERMAN** hit the international spotlight when his graduation film, *See You at Wembley, Frankie Walsh,* won the Best Student Film Academy Award in 1987. He made his full-length feature debut in 1992 with the comedy *Blame It on the Bellboy*, starring Dudley Moore, Patsy Kensit, Bryan Brown and Alison Steadman, but it was his critically acclaimed *Brassed Off* which launched his film career. The film, which starred Pete Postlethwaite, Ewan McGregor and Tara Fitzgerald, about a group of miners overcoming the odds to become national brass band champions, opened the Sundance Film Festival in 1996. It went on to become a British commercial hit and won the French César for Best European Film in 1998, the Peter Sellers Award for Comedy, and the Writers' Guild Award for Best Screenplay.

He followed it up with *Little Voice*, based on the play by Jim Cartwright and starring Jane Horrocks, Brenda Blethyn, Michael Caine and Ewan McGregor. It not only became a smash hit in the UK, grossing over £8m, but also won critical plaudits around the world, including a Best Supporting Actress Oscar nomination for Blethyn and a Golden Globe Best Actor Award for Caine.

Herman is also an accomplished songwriter, having written a string of hits for British band The Christians.

Mark Herman

PURELY
BELTER

FILMFOUR 4

First published 2000 by FilmFour Books
an imprint of Macmillan Publishers Ltd
25 Eccleston Place, London SW1W 9NF
Basingstoke and Oxford

www.macmillan.com

Associated companies throughout the world

ISBN 0 7522 1904 9

9 8 7 6 5 4 3 2 1

A CIP catalogue record for this book is available from the British Library.

Photographs by Simon Mein
Typeset by Ben Cracknell Studios
Printed in Great Britain by Mackays of Chatham plc, Chatham, Kent

Introduction
by Mark Herman

I'd heard it was the story of two kids saving up for Newcastle United season tickets. I'd just spent the last year – never mind the previous and depressing thirty-five – watching my team, Hull City, hack their way to safety at the bottom of the basement division, so football wasn't exactly high on my list of entertaining subject matter for films. Season tickets at Hull City feel more like life sentences, so it was with some reluctance in spring 1999 that I read a proof copy of Jonathan Tulloch's *The Season Ticket.* However, it was with great relief, and an abundance of pleasure, that I very soon realized it had precious little to do with that (occasionally) Beautiful Game. The two main characters, Gerry and Sewell, were brilliantly drawn, at the same time very funny and very tragic, and the world they inhabited appealed to the film-maker in me. Football, yes, was a broad backdrop, but like *Brassed Off*, which one could enjoy without any particular fondness for brass band music (thank God), a love or knowledge of football was similarly irrelevant here. Again, this was a story of the disenfranchised, the Unlucky in Life, the struggle for respect, the triumph of hope over adversity, told by Jonathan in a very warm and emotional way. Most importantly of all, this was a story about people, not the people's game.

I had recently adapted *Little Voice* from stage to screen, but this was the first time I had ever contemplated adapting a novel. Some of Jonathan's best writing brilliantly describes the world in which these kids lived. Beautifully written, a treat to read, but a bugger to film. Whereas a stage play usually has a certain inbuilt drama, one that can be adapted to film without too much difficulty, a novel of this descriptive style poses different problems, and the dramatic structure in this case was not so easy to transfer. More than anything else, I had fallen in love with the dialogue and relationship between these two boys, and that was the foundation on which I built the screenplay. During the four- or five-draft process of adaptation, I changed the book's original structure and storyline quite significantly, mainly to make the piece more accessible to a movie audience. At the same time, and this is often the difficult bit, the concepts, notions, intentions and atmosphere of Jonathan's work were (I hope) maintained and protected. Having had my own work adapted in the past, I'm well aware of the discomfort (to put it mildly) involved when some stranger starts meddling with your work, and the period during which Jonathan was reading the proposed screenplay was probably even more excruciating for me than it was for him. His phone call relaying his happy approval was a colossal relief.

FilmFour's readiness to solely finance a film without stars was an added pressure. Not that I'm complaining, of course. I think their backing of the project was a tribute to the material, but with that comes the enormous responsibility of making that material work. And in order to make it work, more than anything else we had to find the right young actors. Casting director Susie Figgis and her assistant trawled the North-East for teenagers capable of playing Gerry and Sewell. They narrowed the field down to about a hundred possibles. A few weeks later we got it down to a handful of probables, and then finally we got it down to Chris Beattie and Greg McLane. A lot of the kids we saw had done a fair bit of television and film, but these two, who had done precious little (if any) of either, shone through. In fact I think it was their lack of experience that made them appeal to me. They weren't as mannered as the more obvious candidates; there was an innocence and freshness about them, a certain unpretentious air that I really liked. Of course, their lack of experience could also prove to be a disadvantage when the cameras began to roll, but I always felt this would be outweighed by their natural talent. These two characters carry the film: they are in virtually every scene, the audience is supposed to fall for them, and it was vital that we cast the right actors. Having now shot and cut the film, I think young Chris and Greg did a truly remarkable job.

As always, the shooting was not without its complications. They say never work with children, animals (or footballers). We had all three. Like a lot of defensive premiership players, we found Alan Shearer very hard to pin down, but when we finally got him he was terrific. He gave his not insubstantial fee to charity, and for a film that highlights greed in sport and cruelly features his own (fictional) bad taste in music, that was a very laudable gesture. Rusty the dog was impeccable, though like many actors I've worked with he needed constant stroking, salivated wildly at lunchtimes and occasionally tried to hump the director. Filming in Tyneside in November was always going to be hard work, short days and brass monkeys, but being in a city that knows how to have a good time, I don't think anybody really noticed.

We were very fortunate – again, I think, testament to Jonathan's story – to attract the services of some wonderful character actors. People of the calibre of Tim Healy, Kevin Whately, Charlie Hardwick, Val McLane, Roy Hudd and the late but great Willie Ross are not easy to get, and they all sprinkle the film with their own individual magic. I turned Jonathan's novel into a screenplay, but that is just paper. It was these people, the rest of the cast, producer Elizabeth Karlsen, and a very loyal and hard-working crew, who turned the screenplay into the film it is.

Of course, the final draft very rarely matches the final cut of a film. Here I've decided to publish the shooting script. I thought this might be of interest to people who have seen the film and who are keen to know how it evolved and changed through the shooting and post-production stages.

After a couple of early screenings, it became clear that we had to change the title. Too many people who hate football adored the film: people who said that, because of the football connotations, they wouldn't want to see a film called *The Season Ticket*. So instead, we plumped for the last words of the film, 'purely belter'. They mean very little to most people, which is what I like about them, and at least they are not misleading.

Now I'm off to see a brand-new drama. One that prompts tears and laughter, a subtle blend of comedy and tragedy, and one that will almost certainly have no football content whatsoever: Hull City v Hartlepool.

CAST

Gerry Chris Beattie
Sewell Greg McLane
Mrs McCarten Charlie Hardwick
Clare Tracy Whitwell
Baby Sheara Kate & Laura Garbutt
Gemma Jody Baldwin
Bridget Kerry Ann Christiansen
Mr McCarten Tim Healy
Mrs Brabin Su Elliott
Matthew Brabin Daniel James Lake
Mr Sewell Roy Hudd
Mr Caird Kevin Whately
Mrs Caird Tracey Wilkinson
Miss Warren Libby Davison
Maureen Val McLane
Ginga Willie Ross
Zak Adam Fogerty
Waterstone's Assistant Jo-Anne Horan
Auntie Maud Anne Orwin
Cashier 1 Rebekah Joy Gilgan
Cashier 2 Lynne Wilmot
Businessman Michael Hodgson
Policeman Bill Gerard
Policeman Phil Swinburn
Magistrate Joyce Gibbs
Vicar Christopher Connel
Old Dear Veronica Twidle
Alan Shearer Alan Shearer
Mally Charlie Richmond

Jimmy Chris Wiper
Bright Boy Richard Dawson
Bright Girl Helen Parker
Darren Adam Moran
Dinner Lady Anna Maria Gascoigne
Janine Joanne Hickson
Kebab Shop Girl Hayley Murray
Mrs Harvey Madaleine Moffatt
Park Worker Brendan Healy
Bingo Caller Billy Fane
Car Park Attendant Trevor Fox
Rusty The Dog Ben

CREW

Written and directed by Mark Herman
Produced by Elizabeth Karlsen
Based on the novel The Season Ticket by
                    Jonathan Tulloch
Executive Producer Stephen Woolley
Director of Photography Andy Collins
Production Designer Don Taylor
Edited by Michael Ellis a.c.e.
Line Producer Cathy Lord
Music composed by Ian Broudie &
                    Michael Gibbs
Costume Designer Jill Taylor
Make-up & hair design Veronica Brebner
Casting Director Susie Figgis

x

1. EXT. BLACK SPACE. NIGHT.

*Under opening credits we see nothing but **pitch
black**. And hear nothing, either, except for the
sound of attempts to restrain breathless
excitement. This is interrupted by regular but
strange scrunching noises. One, then two, then a
third. Finally, a young male voice:*

GERRY   Ha'way, Sewell man, I want straight edges,
y'know? Watch what you're doing, man.

SEWELL   What you on about? It's pitch bloody black, man!

GERRY   Here.

*There is the sound of hurried clumsy fiddling,
then the strike of a match. For a fleeting
moment, lit by the golden flare, we see the faces
of two teenagers, one small, GERRY [15] and
one tall, SEWELL [17]. They wear identical black
ski-hats. Almost before we have taken in this
image, the match blows out. Black again.*

GERRY   (CONT.) Agh, shite, that was me last one an' all.

SEWELL   Aye well, bang go your straight edges. You'll
have to make do with zigzag, like.

Scrunch.

GERRY   Ha'way, it'll look daft, man.

SEWELL   Gerry man, *doin'* this is daft.

GERRY   What you on about? We're entitled. It's ours.
           Belongs to the people of Newcastle, this.

SEWELL   No, it doesn't.

           Scrunch.

GERRY   Aye, well it should do. Used to.

           We hear some distant voices, a dog barks.

GERRY   (CONT.) Ha'way, activity. Step on it, Sewell man.

SEWELL   Nearly done, I think.

GERRY   Any road, if we cannet *be* a part of it, we may as
           well *take* a part of it, eh?

SEWELL   Oh aye, I know. 'It's not the winning that counts,
           it's the taking part.' Jesus, I need some bloody
           light, man.

           *As if on cue, suddenly the world is lit up. Or, at
           least, a football stadium is. The floodlights of St
           James's Park, home of Newcastle United, are so
           bright they almost blind GERRY and SEWELL.
           They are identically dressed in tatty black*

tracksuit bottoms (three stripes), sweatshirts and white trainers, but SEWELL wears a heavy jacket, the sort that football managers and substitutes wear on the touch-line. They are frozen for a moment like rabbits caught in the headlights. There is distant shouting and they see three SECURITY MEN and a barking Alsatian dog running towards them. SEWELL drops the spade and helps GERRY heave up the near-perfect square yard of turf he has cut from behind the goal-line. GERRY lifts it onto his head, and the camera follows them with urgency as they both leg it for freedom across the pitch, leaving behind them the residue square of brown soil that slightly mars the otherwise billiard-table-perfect rectangle. Main title:

'PURELY BELTER'

2. EXT. MCCARTEN HOUSE (1). DAY.

A huge close-up of a blooming flower, its vibrant sun-drenched red fills the screen. A title:

'Summer'

The camera pulls back to reveal that the flower is one of several bordering a very recognizable square of grass that has been laid in the otherwise drab backyard of a terrace house, an

*oasis of green in the grey. From inside, we can
hear a baby crying. The crying, however, is soon
drowned out by a woman's hacking cough. We
see rows of redundant dock cranes behind the
terrace as the camera rises above the noise, and
towards the back bedroom window:*

3. INT. GERRY'S BEDROOM. MCCARTEN HOUSE (1). DAY.

*The hot sun streams in through the curtains and
down onto a bed where GERRY has a pillow
pulled over his head to block out the noise of
baby-cry and woman-cough. Then suddenly it all
stops. Beautiful silence. GERRY emerges from
under the pillow, hardly believing the total hush.
To enhance the moment, he reaches down to the
ashtray that is last night's lager can and selects
the tab-end with most potential, strikes a match
and inhales. He is instantly seized by a racking
cough and doubles up, veins bulging. During an
intake of breath, he hears from below:*

MAM   Gerry pet! Sewell's here!

4. INT. LIVING ROOM. MCCARTEN HOUSE (1). DAY.

*His mother, MAM, bears a clear resemblance to
Gerry. A small woman, her dyed hair is almost*

4

*proud of its morning messiness. Her teeth are
alternately yellow and brown, her eyes seem big,
but her body worn. She sits, smoking, on a
threadbare armchair holding a naked baby,
SHEARA. SEWELL, again immersed in his bench-
coat, wholly inappropriate on this hot summer
day, sits opposite her. In the adjoining kitchen,
Gerry's sister CLARE has her sweatshirt sleeves
rolled up as she digs through shopping bags in a
mad search for nappies. She is tall, unlike the
others, with a thin face as white as asbestos.*

MAM   Take your coat off, Sewell pet, you look like
        you've been lagged.

SEWELL I'm all right, ta, Mrs McCarten.

MAM   You must be sweating rivers in there, big lad.
        What with all that blubber.

SEWELL I'm all right, Mrs McCarten, honest. I won't feel
        the benefit, y'know.

        *MAM frowns her confusion, then smiles a
        sympathetic smile. GERRY, still donning a
        T-shirt, runs down the stairs and in.*

GERRY   Areet, Mam.

        Leans and pushes his face at his niece.

5

GERRY   (CONT.) Areet, our Sheara. Jesus, she *stinks*, man!

MAM   So did you, man Gerry.

GERRY   Not like that I never. I'd remember.

CLARE   You still do sometimes.

GERRY   Areet, Clare, what you up to?

CLARE   Brought Mam her shopping, like.

GERRY   Still no Bridget then?

MAM   No.

MAM glances across at the family photo on the mantelpiece of seemingly happier times. A group shot of Mam, Dad, Clare, Gerry and Bridget. Almost to herself:

MAM   (CONT.) … Three weeks now.

CLARE   Don't ye fret, Mam, she'll be back.

There is a definite feeling that nobody in the room believes that. The pause is suddenly punctured as MAM starts coughing again, which in turn sets SHEARA off crying again. MAM struggles to hand SHEARA over to GERRY.

GERRY is uncomfortable with a screaming stinking baby in his arms but it is only a second before CLARE comes in and pushes a bottle full of orange squash into her mouth and the crying immediately subsides. SEWELL watches MAM fighting for air until, eventually, her coughing stops also.

SEWELL   You all right, Mrs McCarten?

MAM   Never better, Sewell son, never better.

GERRY   Ha'way then, man Sewell, are we gannin?

          SEWELL gets up to join GERRY.

CLARE   Where are you off?

MAM   Wouldn't be school by any chance, would it, pet?

GERRY   I told you, Mam, I'm studying at the University o'Life, me.

MAM   University o'Life, my arse. Sewell man, cannet *you* talk some sense into the...?

          She looks SEWELL up and down, shakes her head.

MAM   (CONT.) ... No, no, I'm asking the wrong person.

5. EXT. ANGEL HILL. DAY.

> GERRY and SEWELL climb up a steep grass hill.
> Behind and below them, the city of Newcastle
> hangs like a backdrop. We see the Tyne and its
> many bridges. GERRY's is a busy walk, swaying
> him nimbly from side to side with his elbows out,
> his head constantly swivelling and searching like
> a lean urban fox. SEWELL follows at a distance
> of half a pace, slanting forward with hunched
> shoulders and wrinkled brow, as though he is
> being led, against his will, by his forehead.
> SEWELL's steps, nearly twice the size of
> GERRY's, appear slow and vague by
> comparison. If GERRY has the look of an urban
> fox, SEWELL's, aided by his bench-coat, is that
> of an overgrown tortoise. As tiny as they are in
> this landscape, we can hear them talking. First
> SEWELL, whose voice is not only muffled by the
> bench-coat, but also has a strange, strangled,
> steadily rising tone.

SEWELL Ha'way, Gerry, admit it. We'll never see the lads
again, us.

GERRY Aye, we will.

SEWELL Haddaway, the only way the likes of us can see
the lads now is on bloody telly. It's fact, man.

On each step, SEWELL's face grows increasingly red.

GERRY   Pack it in, man Sewell.

SEWELL makes an inarticulate but questioning noise.

GERRY   (CONT.) You're holding your breath again, man. Pack it in.

SEWELL exhales like a pricked balloon, the expelled air throwing him forward.

SEWELL   Aagh, Gerry man – I was trying to beat my record. Up to the top here without a breath. I nearly had it an'all. No, I'm telling you, we'll never see them again. Not in the flesh, like.

GERRY   Aye, we will.

SEWELL   How, like?

5A. EXT. ANGEL OF THE NORTH. DAY.

GERRY sits on a freshly mown mound of grass. He lights a suspiciously fat roll-up, pulls hard on it. There is a slightly glazed look in his eye as he stares middle distance towards the city. The camera creeps in on him.

GERRY   I can see it now, Sewell. We'll get in there dead
early, man. To soak up the atmosphere, like. And
we'll buy us a big cup o'tea each, eh? Two
sugars. *Dead* milky, like. And when the Toon
come out we'll get up and go bananas, you
know, like you do.

Sewell sits down next to him.

GERRY   (CONT.) And then they'll kick off, and we'll just be
there, dead cushdy like, sitting in our seats,
sipping our tea, watching our lads... Belter, eh?
Purely *belter*.

*SEWELL has been slowly nodding his head in
considered agreement. The nods now turn into
shakes.*

SEWELL   What you on about, Gerry man?

*GERRY speaks the words slowly and with great
relish as though they are a mouthful of
appetizing food:*

GERRY   Season tickets.

*SEWELL stares at him, uncertain whether he is
joking or just a few sandwiches short of a picnic.
GERRY stands and paces about, as if gestating
some grand plan.*

SEWELL   Season tickets? *Us?*

GERRY   Why aye, why not, like?

SEWELL   Well, for one, they don't hand them out on the
         Social, y'know? They're about five hundred
         pound, like. Each.

GERRY   Aye, so?

SEWELL   So. We're about five hundred pound short, like.
         Each.

GERRY   Aye, so? You know what you and me need,
         Sewell man?

SEWELL   Aye, about a thousand pound, by the sound of it.

GERRY   A mission.

SEWELL   A *mission*? Bloody miracle, more like.

GERRY   Ha'way, Sewell man, what d'you say? Owt we
         can think up for mekkin money, we do. And we
         save it all up, y'know? We stop chucking it away
         an'all. Pack in the tabs, pack in the tac here, no
         booze, no glue. We put all that money aside, like,
         along with all we get from thieving and
         twocking… and benefits, and save it all up for
         our *season tickets*. There's a while yet till the
         season starts. We can do it *easy*, man.

SEWELL   You're not even *on* benefits, Gerry man, you're still at school. Supposed to be, any road.

GERRY   Aye, but we're a *team*, Sewell man, right? A team on a mission. We cannet fail, man. Specially with *this* lass looking after us.

SEWELL   Eh?

GERRY   The Guardian Angel of twockers, like. She'll see us through.

> *SEWELL's neck emerges for the first time as he twists to look up above him. A wide shot. It has to be wide to incorporate the colossal girdered wingspan of the Angel of the North, which towers above the whole area like an immense watchful giant, spreading its protective wings over the entire North-East. It certainly dwarfs GERRY and SEWELL, tiny pathetic figures by comparison. The golden light of early evening shines on the rust statue as, below it, Gerry takes one last drag from his smoke and offers it to Sewell to finish.*

SEWELL   No, ta. I've given up, me. I'm on a mission.

> *Gerry smiles. SEWELL grins back. They look towards the blue dusk of the city. Just before Gerry chucks it.*

SEWELL   (CONT.) Oh areet, one last drag, man.

6. EXT. MUD FLATS. BOATYARD. DAY.

Dawn breaks over the enormous derelict loading jetty and the mud banks of the River Tyne below. Their flat perfection has been broken by a trail of deep footprints and we find, at the end of it, SEWELL, his grin long gone now as he struggles knee-deep in the smelly, glutinous, ashen-coloured mud. Embedded in it with him are all manner of artefacts – bicycle frames, shopping trolleys, sinks, rusted industrial chains, car wheels, even an entire car sunk up to its roof. SEWELL is tugging at an old toilet. GERRY, whose grin is strangely broad for this time in the morning, smiles even more as every step that SEWELL takes sinks him progressively deeper into the slime.

SEWELL   Ha'way, Gerry, give us a hand, man!

GERRY   Haddaway, man, one of us has got to look respectable if we're going to sell anything. First rule of scrap dealing: You might make money out of shite but you cannet smell of the stuff.

SEWELL   I cannet shift it, man.

The toilet is wedged deep in the mud. SEWELL tugs and tugs but it won't budge. Finally, losing his patience, SEWELL gives it one last almighty heave. His hands slip and he falls back. There's a

*dull splat as he hits the mud headlong. GERRY is
in hysterics. SEWELL manages to stagger
upright once more, caked in shit.*

GERRY   Ha'way, stop fannying about now, Sewell man,
the tide's coming in.

SEWELL   What you on about? Tide's not in for hours, man.

*As SEWELL frantically treads mud, GERRY
stands on the top step looking down at his friend
complacently.*

GERRY   No, but it's a spring tide today, y'know. Biggest
of the month. Comes up quick, covers all this
mud, mind. Oh aye, they find all sorts when they
dredge this lot after a spring tide, y'know? Cats,
dogs... humans. All drowned, like. Struggled
valiantly, like you, but couldn't get free. All found
in the same shape... Like Subbuteo goalies,
y'know?

Stands upright, reaching for the sky.

SEWELL   Piss off and just get us out, man, I'm trapped.

He is floundering in the stuff.

SEWELL   (CONT.) Ha'way, man Gerry, I'm sinking,
man!GERRY Aye, they're pure evil, them spring
tides.

In his panic, SEWELL falls forward again,
breaking his fall with his hands. GERRY comes
nonchalantly down the steps with a long wide
plank and drops it, splat, onto the mud.

GERRY   (CONT.) Watch, mud monster, and ye shall learn.
         Practical science, like.

He begins to walk carefully along the plank.

GERRY   (CONT.) If you'd stopped at school you'd know
         these things. I'll get the bog out first, then come
         back for you.

SEWELL   *Eh!?*

GERRY   Second rule of scrap dealing: Leave the real
         shite till last.

7. EXT. MONCUR ROAD (BRABIN HOUSE). DAY.

The old toilet is in a similarly mud-caked old
shopping trolley. It precedes GERRY and
SEWELL round a corner as they push it into a
terraced street like hundreds of others round
here. Suddenly, to SEWELL's huge
embarrassment, GERRY begins to shout, very
loudly. So loud it might just be heard in
Middlesbrough.

GERRY   RAG and BOOONE!! Any ould RAAG and
         BOOOOONE!!

         *SEWELL slides his head into the depths of his
         muddy bench-coat.*

SEWELL   What you *doing*, man?

GERRY   What they all do! Any ould RAAAG and
         BOOOOOONE!!

SEWELL   You're embarrassing, man.

GERRY   *I'm* embarrassing? Look at *you*! H'way, d'you
         want this season ticket or not?

SEWELL   Course I do, man, more than…

GERRY   RAAAG an' BOOAAAN!! Any ould RAAAAG an'
         BOOOOAAN!!

MRS BRABIN   You're not the usual.

         *A woman, MRS BRABIN, is watching them from
         in front of her doorway, her arms tightly folded
         and her mouth clamped, vice-like, around a
         cigarette. She has short jagged dyed-blonde hair
         and wears dirty white towelling jogging trousers
         and sweat-top. Her mouth is all gums and her
         words have to force their way past the cigarette.*

MRS BRABIN   (CONT.) Does Terry know you're doing this?

GERRY looks non-plussed

MRS BRABIN   (CONT.) Y'know? Terry? The gadgie who
                        normally comes round.

GERRY   Terry! Y'mean *Uncle* Terry. Why aye.

MRS BRABIN   You lying bastards. Haddaway, come in,
                        lads, I've got something for you.

She looks at SEWELL's coat.

MRS BRABIN   (CONT.) Eee, is that the new look, then?

SEWELL   Eh?

MRS BRABIN   Pebble-dash? You look like you've been
                        stood at the arse end of an elephant, you.

8. EXT. YARD. BRABIN HOUSE. DAY.

*Ten dogs of different shapes and sizes forage
around the yard, scampering in and out of the
house. As MRS BRABIN leads the boys in, she
swings at the dogs.*

MRS BRABIN   Away, *you bastards!* They're my son's. I
                wouldn't mind, but it's a new one every week.
                Fourteen of 'em there was in the house last
                night. They stink an'all. Crap all over. But I can't
                do owt about it. He goes radge if I mention it.
                Anyways, lads, this is what you can take. It's
                knackered, like.

                She indicates an old fridge. GERRY and SEWELL
                glance at each other. It may be 'knackered' to
                her, but to them it's jackpot time. It's certainly a
                step up from the well-soiled bog.

9. EXT. MONCUR ROAD (BRABIN HOUSE). DAY.

                MRS BRABIN watches GERRY and SEWELL
                'walk' the fridge down the front step and out into
                the street. As the fridge hits the pavement, the
                door swings open and a DOG jumps out. MRS
                BRABIN hurls a handful of insults at it as it jumps
                up at SEWELL, who tries to pet it.

SEWELL   Now then, you canny hound, you!

MRS BRABIN   Get hold of the bastard, you, quick! Shite!

                But the dog is off, running up the street. SEWELL
                laughs at it, but MRS BRABIN suddenly looks
                decidedly worried, almost in a panic. The dog
                scampers friskily round the corner, making

SEWELL laugh even more, and then out of sight.
MRS BRABIN frets.

MRS BRABIN   (CONT.) He'll *murder* me he will. His
                favourite, that. He'll go mad if that one's not in
                when he gets back.

SEWELL   What's he doing in the fridge but? He's a hound,
            man, not a bloody penguin.

MRS BRABIN   That one'd be in the microwave if I had
                one. See you, lads...

                She looks up the street with, quite literally, a
                'dog-gone' expression.

MRS BRABIN   (CONT.) ...if I live.

SEWELL   See you. Ta.

                She shuts the door and GERRY and SEWELL lift
                the fridge onto the shopping trolley and begin to
                wheel it down the road with difficulty. They have
                only staggered a few yards when they see,
                coming down the road from the other direction,
                a frightening sight: with three dogs around his
                feet, a boy approaches. He wears only a pair of
                baggy shorts, his scant body yellow in the
                sunlight, his overlong arms an endless cordage
                of sinew and bone, culminating in horrifically
                long fingernails. His filthy face is scarred and

*spotty, he has eyes that seem like they died
before he was born, he has a tattoo of what
looks like the teeth of a Rottweiler on his
completely bald head. He has as few charming
attributes as he has teeth, which are pointlessly
but frighteningly braced. It is MATTHEW. He
passes GERRY and SEWELL, his dead eyes
barely registering their presence, let alone that
of his (ex-)fridge. GERRY and SEWELL know of
MATTHEW, but seeing him at such close
quarters is nonetheless still alarming. MATTHEW
opens his front door and announces his arrival
with a grunt.*

10. INT. MCCARTEN HOUSE (1). DAY.

*A similarly incomprehensible noise comes out of
baby SHEARA, difficult to say from which end.
She struggles to put one foot in front of the other
as she aims for MAM on the settee. MAM smiles
at her, holding out her hands.*

MAM   Ha'way, pet, say something, say something for
          your nana. Ha'way, ha'way.

          SHEARA belches, then collapses.

MAM   (CONT.) Agh, you take after your grandad, you.
          No words, just all dribble and puke.

She picks her up and holds her softly.

MAM   (CONT.) Don't you cry. Nana's here, pet. Nana'll always be here for you. Shall I sing to you?

The phone starts ringing beside her. She ignores it

MAM   (CONT.) Shall I sing to you, my little Sheara?

She sings, beautifully:

MAM   (CONT.) *'Ah cannet get to my love if ah should dee The water of Tyne runs between him and me...'*

CLARE comes through to answer the phone.

MAM   (CONT.) Leave it. *'...And here ah must sit with a tear in my e'e...'*

CLARE   Phone calls aren't always bad, y'know?

MAM   Clare pet, I'd know if I'd won the bloody lottery. *'...Both sighin' and sickly my true love to see...'* No, it'll be the Social. Or the school. Or the bank.

CLARE   ...Or Bridget?

MAM looks at the phone.

MAM   Or your dad?

The thought makes CLARE return to the kitchen.

MAM   *'Oh where is the boatman, my bonny hinny*
        Oh where is the boatman, bring him to me...'

11. EXT. BANKS OF THE TYNE. DAY.

We see the River Tyne and, pushing the trolley
along its banks, GERRY and SEWELL.

MAM   (O/S) *'...To ferry me over the Tyne to my hinny*
        And ah shall remember the boatman and thee.'

11A. EXT. STEPS. BANKS OF THE TYNE. DAY.

GERRY and SEWELL look even more knackered
than the bog and fridge respectively as they
struggle to push the trolley along the pathway
under one of the rail bridges.

SEWELL Jesus, I wish we'd had that cup o'tea the old
        wife back there offered us. I'm gasping, me.

GERRY   I knew you fancied her. I could see what you
        were thinking when you watched her sucking on
        that ciggie.

        They laugh in the heat.

SEWELL   And I'm starving, man.

GERRY   When we get our season tickets, Sewell man.
That's the time for tea and snacks...and blow-
jobs from Mrs Brabin.

They laugh again, making steering the trolley
even harder.

12. EXT. GINGA'S WAREHOUSE. DAY.

GERRY and SEWELL are breathless and
exhausted as they wheel the bog and fridge
down a cobbled road under arches and into an
area of scrapyards and junk garages. There is
junk that's junk and there's junk that's real junk,
and the stuff outside these places is real junk.
GERRY looks dubious.

GERRY   You're sure this felluh's gonna buy this stuff?

SEWELL   Why aye. Give it a knock then, man.

GERRY still holds the fridge steady as he knocks
on the insert door of an arches lock-up.

GERRY   Who is he, like?

SEWELL   Ginga? Just one of me dad's old mates.

GERRY   Agh, hell, man, that's all we need.

SEWELL   What d'you mean by that, like?

GERRY   Look, no offence to your old man or any of his
            mates, but ... well, man Sewell... They're all as
            skint as we are.

SEWELL   Ginga's not skint. He's made a mint out of scrap.

GERRY   Oh aye, this'll just be one of his many branches
            nationwide, like, eh?

SEWELL   You'll have to knock louder. I think he's getting
            deaf, old Ginga.

GERRY   Aye well, tycoons cannet have everything. Hold
            on to this then...

            *GERRY takes his other arm away to pound on the
            door. Still no reply. SEWELL, and the trolley,
            begin to buckle under the extra weight. SEWELL's
            strength finally gives way and the trolley falls
            over, the fridge and the bog falling to the ground.
            The fridge door falls off and the bog breaks into
            several pieces. We hear a voice from above:*

GINGA   Hello?

            *Up above them, leaning out of a loft loading
            door, is GINGA. GINGA is an old man whose hair*

is flamingly ginger. His beard seems to totally fill his face, leaving only the smallest of portholes for his eyes, mouth and nose (the hair in which is also ginger).

SEWELL Ginga! We've brought you something.

GINGA looks down, unimpressed, at the now separate sections of the already useless old fridge, and the smashed toilet.

13. INT. GINGA'S WAREHOUSE. DAY.

The inside of this first-floor warehouse is totally unlike anything the lads have ever seen before. Every single object in it, every single fixture and fitting, every single ornament and utility has been salvaged. The waste of Tyne and Wear is resurrected here. GERRY and SEWELL sit, exhausted, on a settee which is the back seat of a car, while GINGA sits opposite them in the passenger's seat. They gaze around the place in wonderment at the massive collection of diverse, and in some cases perverse, junk. A corner of the warehouse, though barely distinguishable from the rest, is Ginga's living quarters – stove, bed, wardrobe etc. He scans the room with them:

GINGA   Aye, things've never been the same since you nippers took up joy-riding. It's been a *godsend*, man.

He pats his passenger seat.

GINGA   (CONT.) You provide all my upholstery. Hey, aren't you Harry Sewell's young'un? How's he doing, your old man?

SEWELL   *(Still gawping in awe)* Champion.

GINGA sees them looking around and grins. He follows their gaze to an elaborate fireplace.

GINGA   Having a good look round, lads? The Mayor of Gateshead used to toast his arse on that, y'know? Ey, talking of toast, you must be canny hot in that snorkel jacket, Harry Sewell's lad.

SEWELL   It's a bench-coat, Ginga.

GINGA   A bent stoat?

GERRY and SEWELL glance at each other.

GERRY   A bench-coat, y'know? A training jacket. Like all them footie managers wear.

GINGA   Fuckin' bandages? What you on about?

*GERRY and SEWELL exchange further looks and
shakes of the head. A pause, then, very loud:*

GERRY   *We've got you some stuff!*

GINGA   Jesus, I'm not deaf, ye know? I know. I saw. A
knackered old fridge and a busted bog.

GERRY   Bit of Super-glu, like, be good as new.

GINGA   Aye. Well, thanks very much, lads.

GERRY   Aye.

SEWELL   Aye.

GINGA   Aye.

*They sit through a cul-de-sac silence. There are
several ticking clocks. After a painful while:*

GINGA   (CONT.) Ah well, it's nice of you lads to bring it
round. You looking for owt else?

A shocked beat.

GERRY   Em... We thought you might pay us, like.

GINGA   Eh? Ha! Me ears, lads, I'm sorry... I thought you
said I might *'pay'* you!

He sees their faces, realizes they did.

GINGA   (CONT.) Oh, hey, I've no *money*, lads. I'm what's
called living beyond the cash economy.

He sees that the lads are crestfallen.

GINGA   (CONT.) Ah, go on then, I'll tell you what. I'll take
the fridge off you in return for anything you see
in here you fancy. But I'm going to have to pass
on the self-assembly shitter, like.

*SEWELL and GERRY, clearly disappointed, look
around. The choice is limitless, though probably
worthless. CUT TO:*

14. EXT. DUNSTON STAITHES JETTY. DUSK.

*GERRY and SEWELL walk back along the lower
tier of the long jetty, their shoulders drooping
from exhaustion and disappointment. It is the
end of a long day.*

GERRY   Well, what a cracking start that was, eh?
Sweating and heaving all day. Carrying cart-
loads of crap all over Tyneside. Yelling at old
money-bags there for an hour. And what do we
get out of it? A fucking *cuckoo clock*!

In the shopping trolley we see the Newcastle United cuckoo clock that GERRY has chosen in exchange for the fridge.

SEWELL   Ha'way, a *Magpie* cuckoo clock.

GERRY   Oh aye, thank Christ for that, eh? Wouldn't want to think we was wasting our time.

SEWELL   Jesus man, I could murder a tab, me.

A bark sounds behind them. Then another one. SEWELL looks round. It is the dog they'd seen trapped in the fridge earlier. It seems to be following them along the jetty. Crouching down, SEWELL extends a hand towards the animal, rubbing his fingers together encouragingly.

SEWELL   (CONT.) Ha'way, it's that hound. Here, boy, come to Sewell.

GERRY   How do you know it's a boy, like?

SEWELL   Look at its bollocks, man. It must have been trailing us.

GERRY   You mean following the stench of your coat.

SEWELL   No, he just likes us, that's all. Here, hound, here.

After a period of doubt, the dog finally takes
another few steps towards SEWELL, its snout
surveying him with rapid sniffs, then suddenly
lets out a yelp and throws itself at him, bundling
him over with its paws and licking him all over.
SEWELL laughs with his wet face.

SEWELL   (CONT.) Ey, I think I'll call it... Rusty.

GERRY   Ha'way, man Sewell, you can't *keep* it, man. It's
that Matthew Brabin's. And you know what a
radgie mad lad *he* is. You saw. He even scares
his own *mam* shitless.

    SEWELL stands up and the dog jumps up at him
    again. Catching hold of his paws, SEWELL
    dances a few steps with the dog.

SEWELL   Look at it, dead intelligent, man.

GERRY   Intelligent? Oh aye. Let's test it out then. Now
then, you smelly hound...

SEWELL   Rusty.

GERRY   Oh yeah... Now then Rusty, you smelly hound.
How many pounds does a season ticket cost?

SEWELL   Ha'way, man, he cannet answer that!

GERRY   He would if he was intelligent. He'd tap the
         number out with his feet.

SEWELL   They're five hundred pound, man. He'd have no
         bloody feet *left*. No, he knows the answer, he's
         just too smart to want to go about on stumps,
         that's all. Here, I'll show you. All right, Rusty
         man, listen. This is Gerry, the brains behind our
         mission to get Toon season tickets, which, as
         you well know, cost five hundred pounds each.
         So, tell us: how many pounds do you think we've
         got so far, like, eh?

         They look at the dog, who doesn't move.

SEWELL   (CONT.) Correct!

GERRY   F'ckoff man, I'm thinking, I'm thinking.

         *They walk in their usual formation back towards
         the big city. SEWELL shoots a glance back at
         Rusty, who stays sitting, watching them go.*

15. EXT. MULTI-STOREY CAR PARK. GATESHEAD. DAY.

         *FADE UP: Another day. GERRY and SEWELL
         wander through the roof-top floor of a multi-
         storey car park. Newcastle, including St James's
         Park, looms behind them.*

GERRY   ...no, I'm telling you, they're worth the ticket
           price alone, the pies. Dead crusty, like...

           *They see A MAN get out of his car and lock it,
           and they move in. SEWELL tries to look hard.*

GERRY   (CONT.) Mind your car for you?

MAN   Eh?

           *The MAN sees SEWELL stroke a finger along the
           side of his shiny car. He sighs and reaches for his
           wallet. GERRY pockets the money and they
           move on.*

SEWELL   They hot, like? The pies?

GERRY   *Piping* hot, man, and proper meat mind, not just
           your usual gristle and gravy. And they've got
           everything, man. Burgers, chips, Bovril, the lot.
           That's it, you see, when you've a season ticket,
           you're into a whole different class, catering-wise.

           A WOMAN gets out of her car.

GERRY   (CONT.) Mind your car for you?

           *The WOMAN sighs at her bad luck and opens
           her bag.*

GERRY   (CONT.) Kids today, y'know, better safe than
           sorry, eh?

They move on.

GERRY   (CONT.) And not just catering-wise, it's *every-wise*. You just get treated different, y'know? It's not just pasties you get, you get respect an'all. It's like a club, y'know? You *belong*. You just wait, man Sewell, it'll be belter.

Another MAN is getting out of his car.

GERRY   (CONT.) Mind your car...

The MAN straightens up to be enormous.

GERRY   (CONT.) ... Mind your car door on your fingers there, pal.

16. EXT. SEWELL FLAT (DUNSTON ROCKET). DAY.

FADE UP: The Dunston Rocket is a grimy tower block on the south side of the Tyne, nicknamed the Rocket for obvious reasons – it looks like one. What look like four concrete tail-fins hold the building up as if it is on a launch pad. SEWELL and his DAD live at the very top.

17. INT. SEWELL'S BEDROOM. SEWELL FLAT. DAY.

Fittingly, the flat is as cramped as a lunar module. We find SEWELL asleep in his messy bedroom. He even uses his bench-coat as an eiderdown. He is woken by the thunk of a cup of tea on his bedside table. He looks up to see it has been delivered by his dad, MR SEWELL. Dressed in his tatty pyjamas, MR SEWELL has a craggy grey face that makes him look improbably old for Sewell's dad.

MR SEWELL   There y'are, son.

SEWELL   Ta, Dad.

As MR SEWELL shuffles away, SEWELL takes a sip of the tea. Then grimaces.

SEWELL   (CONT.) Dad? Did you make this from the tap?

MR SEWELL   Aye, son, is it all right?

SEWELL   Hot's the one on the *right*, Dad.

MR SEWELL   *(Tuts at himself)* Agh, what am I like, eh? I'll make you another.

SEWELL   No, you're all right, Dad, I'm off out.

MR SEWELL   *(As he leaves)* You're never *in* these days, son. Oh aye, I'll forget me head in a minute, there's someone at the door for you.

SEWELL   Eh?

SEWELL looks through his open bedroom door and sees the front door, also open, and sitting there, RUSTY. SEWELL frowns his amazement, then takes a quick sniff of his bench-coat, which explains a great deal.

18. EXT. STRAWBERRY LANE. DAY.

As rush-hour traffic queues, we see GERRY and SEWELL squeedgie-cleaning windscreens. They chat as they sponge, with blatantly dirty water. St James's Park looms behind them.

GERRY   Ha'way, man, will ye stop ganning on about tabs.

SEWELL   I'm gagging, man. Aye but, will we have one, eh? In our seats, like? To go with the cuppa, like?

GERRY   Aye, maybe. At half-time, y'know? Light up and stretch our legs. Or maybe we won't smoke at all, like.

SEWELL   Aye, or then again... Maybe we'll light up one tab after another, smoke ourselves *mortal*, man.

GERRY   Aye, maybe. And you know what? No one can say a word about it. Cos they'll be *our* seats. No one else's, just *ours*.

He holds a hopeful hand out to DRIVER.

GERRY   (CONT.) There you go.

DRIVER   Get lost, son, I can't see a bloody thing now.

The car drives on. We hear a shout from another one.

DRIVER 2   Hey! Is that thing yours?

We see RUSTY lifting his leg on a previously clean hubcap. FADE.

19. INT. 'LIQUID' CLUB. BIGG MARKET. NIGHT.

A close-up of baby SHEARA, whose peaceful sleep is suddenly and savagely wrecked by the thunderous intro to some techno blare which shakes her chubby cheeks. We see her virtually blasted out of her nappy, her suddenly widened eyes confused by the flashing coloured lights which a wide shot reveals are from the ceiling of some packed 'Shaggers'-type pub on Bigg Market. She is propped up between GERRY and SEWELL. Although it's the kind of pub where you'd be overdressed in a T-shirt, SEWELL is still stubbornly wrapped in his bench-coat, but this isn't why he feels uncomfortable. The music is so loud they yell at each other at the tops of their voices, veins bulging, but we can only just hear them:

SEWELL   It's not right, man Gerry, bringing her here!

GERRY   Haddaway, man, we can't turn down a spot of babby-sitting! A fiver's a fiver!

SEWELL shakes his head, then digs out a can of Orange Tango.

SEWELL   Aye well, I got her this!

GERRY   Good, we'll give it her when she starts crying. That's them trying to tell you they're thirsty.

SEWELL   Or that they've done a shite.

On cue, SHEARA immediately starts crying. GERRY and SEWELL look at each other.

GERRY   Think positive, man, she could be thirsty.

With a hopeful nod, SEWELL hurriedly opens the can.

SEWELL   Here you go, babby.

He tries pouring it in, nearly choking baby.

SEWELL   (CONT.) Ha'way, youngster, take a drink.

The baby flails a hand, cries even harder.

SEWELL   (CONT.) Maybe she just doesn't like Tango. I'll go
         back and get a Vimto. Bairns love Vimto.

         *We see SHEARA and that hugely content face
         that all nappy-filling babies have. There is an
         audible collective complaint from all around.*

GERRY   She's not thirsty, Sewell man.

SEWELL   Eh?

GERRY   Jesus, man, can you not smell it?

SEWELL   Smell what?

         *There is commotion in the far end of the pub,
         where a bunch of scantily clad LASSES have just
         come in. They are welcomed by the customary,
         predictable cheered chorus of male approval. A
         look of terrified recognition takes over GERRY's
         face:*

GERRY   Jesus, man, it's our Clare!

         *CLARE looks happy and relaxed, presumably
         partly because she knows her baby is in safe,
         capable hands back home. GERRY and SEWELL
         and (involuntarily) SHEARA suddenly duck into
         the crowd. They begin the hard work of getting
         out of there, weaving a crouched path through
         the crowd.*

20. INT. BIGG MARKET. GENTS'. NIGHT.

The Bigg Market Gents' toilet is a mass of young lads, but they part quickly on command:

GERRY   Gangway, lads, gangway! And for God's sake breathe through your mouths!!

There are several understandable complaints as GERRY plonks SHEARA in a basin. He tears off the heavy brown nappy and waves it in the air:

GERRY   (CONT.) Ugh... ugh... uhh... Get upwind all of you!

(He quickly lobs it into the toilet, and yells at SEWELL.)

GERRY   (CONT.) Sewell! Rip some of that off, will you, quick?

GERRY nods urgently to the filthy hand-towel roller.

(SCENE 21 DELETED)

22. INT. TOON TAKE-AWAY. NIGHT.

SEWELL, holding SHEARA, who gleefully rattles the ring-pull inside a can of lager, stands behind GERRY in the queue at the counter.

GERRY   Aye, three Gazza Specials... one with not too
             much chilli on... For the bairn, like.

             The customer in front turns to leave.

GEMMA   Hiya, Gerry, areet?

GERRY   Aye, areet, Gemma.

             *GEMMA's hair is an unruly explosion of blonde
             peroxide with the roots showing dark. Her face is
             pretty despite a lean, pinched look that gives her
             the appearance of somebody much older and
             more worldly-wise than she actually is. Her scant
             skirt and T-shirt have the same effect.*

GEMMA   Eeh, Sewell man! Haven't seen you for ages,
             man... You up to owt?

             She sees SHEARA.

GEMMA   (CONT.) Eeh, bloody hell man, you *have* been!

GERRY   It isn't Sewell's, man Gemma, it's our Clare's.

GEMMA   Oh aye. Eeh, canny! Aah, she's got a rattle an'all.

             She laughs. SEWELL likes her laugh.

GEMMA   (CONT.) What's she called?

GERRY   Sheara.

GEMMA   Ah, not another Sheara, they're *everywhere*,
         man. Aaaah. Well, I wish she was mine.

         *GEMMA smiles, then realizes she hasn't
         introduced the man mountain next to her. An
         enormous bruiser of a bloke, considerably older
         than her, the proverbial brick shit-house. He is
         ZAK.*

GEMMA   (CONT.) You know Zak?

         ZAK exchanges nods with GERRY and SEWELL.

GEMMA   (CONT.) Goal-minder for Sunderland Chiefs?
         We're out celebrating, like.

GERRY   Celebrating?

GEMMA   Aye. Look.

         She flaunts a ring on her finger.

GERRY   Canny.

SEWELL   *(Unimpressed)* Aye, canny.

         And with precious little joy:

SEWELL   (CONT.) When's the happy day, like?

GEMMA   End o'next year sometime, soon as I'm sixteen.
         Ey! Yous two are brilliant. Looking after the bairn.
         I'd say you were a 'new man', Sewell pet, if it
         wasn't for the 'old coat', like!

         *He's not sure if it's a compliment. She smiles at
         him with affection.*

GEMMA   (CONT.) Ha'way, I'll see you around, lads, eh?

KEBAB MAN   Three Gazzas.

         *GEMMA and ZAK leave. GERRY hands over a
         £10 note as SEWELL watches GEMMA through
         the window.*

GERRY   Agh, man, you don't still fancy her, do you?

SEWELL   Well, don't you, like?

GERRY   Not when she's gannin oot with a gorilla, no.

         The KEBAB MAN gives him four coins change.

GERRY   (CONT.) Hey, and the rest, man.

KEBAB MAN   Eh?

GERRY   I gave you a twenty.

KEBAB MAN   No, you never.

GERRY   I did.

KEBAB MAN   You didn't.

SEWELL   He did.

GERRY   Jesus, I don't see 'em that often. I know what
         they bloody look like, man.

         The eyes lock, four to two. Eventually, the
         KEBAB MAN gives way and hands GERRY
         another tenner.

23. INT. GERRY'S BEDROOM. MCCARTEN HOUSE (1). DAY.

         Slow FADE UP on a shot of GERRY, same pose
         as the earlier scene, fast asleep in bed. He is
         completely at peace until his face is suddenly
         drenched by the mad licking tongue of RUSTY. It
         catapults him reluctantly from the Land of Nod.

GERRY   Fucking Jesus, man! When are you going to get
         rid of that minging mutt?

SEWELL   I can't.

GERRY   Christ, man Sewell, he's not *yours*! He belongs to
         frigging *psycho bollocks*! Any road, what do you
         want this early in the morning?

SEWELL   It's afternoon.

GERRY   All right, this early in the afternoon.

SEWELL   To count our money, like.

GERRY   We agreed, Sewell man, no counting it until first day of the season.

SEWELL   Aye, I know.

Sewell's failure to expand causes it to dawn on GERRY. It is the first day of the season. He leaps out of bed.

24. INT. BRIDGET'S ROOM. MCCARTEN HOUSE (1). DAY.

Bridget's bedroom has a lived-in feel to it. There is a Garbage poster on the wall and various other signs of her existence, but no actual Bridget. GERRY pulls various clutter out of a cupboard and places it on the floor.

SEWELL   Why do you keep it in Bridget's room, like?

GERRY   Secrecy, Sewell man. We agreed, no one's to know. And no one ever comes in here.

SEWELL   What, not even your Bridget, like?

GERRY doesn't answer.

SEWELL   (CONT.) Is she all right, Bridget?

GERRY   I don't know... We've not seen her since... You
         know... for a while, like.

         *GERRY places a wallpaper-covered shoebox on
         the floor. SEWELL reaches down to lift its lid.
         GERRY smacks his hand away.*

GERRY   (CONT.) Hands off that, man!

SEWELL   Is that not it?

GERRY   No, that's...our Bridget's... special box. You
         know, her... private things, like. Here you are,
         this is the one.

         *GERRY undoes some newspaper wrapping and
         reveals a large 'Toon Army' biscuit tin. He tries to
         prise off the lid, but can't. He hands it over to
         SEWELL.*

GERRY   (CONT.) Here, you're the brawn, man, get that
         off.

         *There is an almost childish excitement on his
         face as SEWELL's fat fingers manage to release
         the lid. He looks into the deep collection of cash.
         But it alarms him, he hands it back.*

45

SEWELL   Here, you're the brains, man, you do the counting.

25. EXT. DOCKSIDE ROAD. MCCARTEN HOUSE (1). DAY.

> *CLARE holds baby SHEARA with one hand and a cigarette with the other. She is wearing a tight red miniskirt and a yellow sweatshirt. Her stiletto-heeled sandals, the same shade of white as her face but without the deep lines of worry, click-clack at speed as she hurries towards the house. The dockyard cranes tower above the grim terrace.*

SEWELL   (O/S) Eighty-five pounds? We did all that for... eighty-five poond?

26. INT. BRIDGET'S ROOM. MCCARTEN HOUSE (1). DAY.

> *SEWELL looks shocked. Pale. He shakes his head in disbelief. GERRY is gathering and stuffing the money back in the tin.*

GERRY   It's a start. Besides, we haven't done that much.

SEWELL   You *what?* We've given up tac, man, and tabs,
         and booze! For *weeks*, man! And we've worked
         our *bollocks* off, man! And you're telling me
         we've only got *eighty-five poond?*

         GERRY looks dejectedly at the money and has to
         accept that his friend, for once, may have a
         point.

GERRY   Aye, you're right. Maybe it's time to get more
         serious. Go into overdrive, like.

SEWELL   I thought we *were* in overdrive, man.

GERRY   Starting from now, Sewell man, we don't waste a
         day, right? Not a minute, not a second. Toon kick
         off today, like, and so do we. Over-overdrive,
         right?

SEWELL   Aye, right, over-overdrive.

27. INT. HALL. MCCARTEN HOUSE (1). DAY.

         GERRY, SEWELL and RUSTY come charging
         downstairs, excited by their new policy.

GERRY AND SEWELL   *'Aah, me lads, ye shoulda seen us*
                   gannin...'

*But they come to a sudden halt at the foot of the
stairs where they come face to face with CLARE.*

CLARE   Areet, our Gerry. Areet, Sewell, hinny?

SEWELL   Aye. You?

GERRY   What's up?

CLARE   Mam rang, Gerry pet. Says she's poorly. I'm
             taking her round to the doctor's.

             *GERRY, suddenly concerned, looks through to
             the living room towards MAM, who, looking even
             more grey than usual, struggles to get up from
             the settee.*

MAM   Don't worry, Gerry lad, just my annual MOT,
             y'know.

CLARE   You not going to school?

MAM   Don't be daft, Clare pet. *I* have more periods
             than he does.

CLARE   So what you doing today?

GERRY   We got plans and that, you know.

CLARE   Have you?

GERRY   Aye.

MAM shakes her head in frustration as she
passes.

MAM   They're up to something, them two. Have been
for weeks. I don't know what it is, but it's not
helping old biddies across road, I know that
much.

CLARE   Look, Gerry pet, be a little angel, eh, and look
after Sheara, will you?

She thrusts the baby into his chest. He grabs
hold.

GERRY   Usual fiver, like?

CLARE   F'ckoff, it's an emergency.

With that, the baby's dumped, and she and Mam
are out of the door. GERRY, clutching the baby,
looks at SEWELL and shrugs a shrug that says
over-overdrive has just gone out of the window.

28. INT. AMUSEMENT ARCADE. CITY CENTRE.
DAY.

GERRY (who holds SHEARA) and SEWELL are
playing a fruit machine.

SEWELL   Nudge two, man.

GERRY   No, one.

He presses nudge button once.

SEWELL   And another, *go on.*

GERRY   *No!*

SHEARA flaps out her chunky hand and slaps the nudge button.

GERRY   (CONT.) Aagh, no, you daft stupid little...

Money begins to kerchunk kerchunk out.

GERRY   (CONT.) ...brilliant bloody *angel, you*!

Even SHEARA giggles. RUSTY is just alarmed by the sound.

29. EXT. METROLAND FUNFAIR. DAY.

A little GIRL tosses a 2p bit into a lucky fountain. GERRY and SEWELL glance at each other for the briefest of moments before both jumping over the fence and wading through the water and trawling for as many coins as they can in the limited time available before they are shouted away. RUSTY looks on in astonishment.

30. EXT. CITY CENTRE. SHOPPING ARCADE. DAY.

GERRY, SEWELL and RUSTY are a pale shadow of the Three Tenors (which is a great deal more than they have in their bucket). Though the acoustics of the ornate arcade do their best to enhance the performance, shoppers actively avoid their slightly biased Nessun Dorma:

GERRY AND SEWELL   'Al'n Sheara, Al'n Sheara... Al'n Sheara-aa-aaaaa Da da da da de DUM de daa!...'

SHEARA cries.

31. EXT. CLARE'S FLAT. BYKER WALL. DAY.

SEWELL holds SHEARA as GERRY rings Clare's doorbell. GERRY sees the net curtain being pulled back by a bare-chested YOUNG LAD. CLARE opens the door, clutching her undone shirt together, looking a bit ruffled.

CLARE   You're back early.

GERRY   You should shag faster. You want us to keep her out another half-hour?

CLARE   Aah, Gerry, pet, will you?

GERRY   You're me sister, course I will. For a fiver.

CLARE   F'ckoff, it's an emergency.

GERRY   Tenner then.

           A beat while CLARE weighs up financial loss versus sexual gratification. Then:

CLARE   Wait there.

           CLARE goes back into her flat. GERRY shouts through.

GERRY   How's Mam?

CLARE   Well, he's given her some pills, like, but she's poorly, man.

           She comes back with a fiver.

CLARE   (CONT.) Make it an hour, eh, Gerry pet?

32. INT. MCCARTEN HOUSE. (1) NIGHT.

GERRY enters. He sees his MAM sitting on the sofa, striking a sad pose, her forehead bowed on to one hand as if she is massaging a headache, a trembling cigarette in the other. The room looks strangely messy.

GERRY   Mam? You all right? Clare says you're not good, like. Hey, where's the telly...? Mam...?

MAM drops her hand and raises her head. She has a swollen, cut lip, with which she painfully pulls on her cigarette. GERRY's eyes close in a mixture of anger and despair.

GERRY   (CONT.) Aagh, no, Dad, *you bastard*!!

MAM   Your bloody Aunty Maud, the old cow. Got a fucking gob on her like the Tyne Tunnel.

GERRY   *(Sits and comforts his mother)* You're all right, Mam, you're all right.

He surveys the room.

GERRY   (CONT.) Jesus, what's he taken this time?

A sudden thought.

GERRY   (CONT.) Hey, did he go into Bridget's room?

MAM   *(Shakes her head and indicates lip)* You don't
           think I got this for nowt, do you?

           GERRY smiles at her pluck. Then sighs heavily.

GERRY   I'll put the kettle on, eh?

MAM   You'll have to go out and buy one first.

           *She smiles bravely. They look at each other
           sadly. Mam shakes her head, tired.*

GERRY   Have you rung the Social?

MAM   What with?

           *GERRY looks at the gap where the phone was.
           They both start laughing. They'd cry if they
           didn't. Finally, MAM puts a hand on the side of
           GERRY's face.*

MAM   (CONT.) Agh, Gerry pet. You skive school, you.
           You nick all sorts... You drink all sorts... You
           smoke I d'know what... And you do nothing, you.
           Except drive your poor mam mad.

           She shakes her head.

MAM   (CONT.) How that bastard ever produced a lad as
           good as you I'll never know.

GERRY smiles an uncertain smile. FADE TO
BLACK.

33. EXT. MCCARTEN BUNGALOW (2). CRAGGS ESTATE. DAY.

The screen is packed with leaves which form a
massive and intricate pattern of yellow and
brown. A title:

'Autumn'

A gust of wind disturbs all the leaves. As it does
so, the camera tilts up to reveal a sea of shabby
run-down prefab bungalows. A big van is outside
one of them and REMOVAL MEN are shifting
household gear in. One of them passes through
frame with the now slightly ragged-looking
square of St James's Park turf.

34. INT. SMALL BEDROOM. MCCARTEN BUNGALOW (2). DAY.

As the thumping of furniture happens elsewhere
in the house, GERRY carefully sticks up and
flattens out the Garbage poster. He digs out of a
bin-liner Bridget's wallpapered shoebox, which
he places in a cupboard, and then also his Toon
biscuit tin of money, which he carefully covers.

35. INT. MAIN ROOM. MCCARTEN BUNGALOW (2). DAY.

> *MAM stares through the net curtains. She seems much more frail than the last time we saw her, seems to have aged more than a mere season. Frail, nervous, and seemingly paying little attention to MAUREEN. MAUREEN is a harassed-looking social worker in her forties. She has an almost permanent brave smile on her face, born of years of futile attempts to look on the bright side. Around them, the REMOVAL MEN continue to shift the McCartens' worldly possessions, turf and all, into their cramped new home.*

MAUREEN I think it's important to, you know... treat it as a... well, a fresh start, like. Clear the decks in your mind and...

> *She shrugs encouragingly.*

MAUREEN (CONT.) ...start again.

MAM Aagh, Maureen, you're like a cracked record, you. You said that last time, and the time before. He'll find us again, he always does. He may be a monster, but he's not a fucking idiot.

MAUREEN He won't find you here.

MAM   Eeh, you're wasted in social work, you. You
           should be a comedian.

MAUREEN   We're only trying to make things better for
           you.

           MAM sighs heavily. GERRY comes in.

MAM   Aye, I know, pet, I know you're doing your best.
           It's just... nothing ever changes, you know?

GERRY   Aye, it does.

           MAUREEN looks at him hopefully.

GERRY   (CONT.) The houses get smaller.

           At the window, MAM stares into the distance.

MAM   Aye, and so does the family.

MAUREEN   Still no word from Bridget?

GERRY   Not going to be now, is there? Now we can't tell
           anyone where we fucking live, like.

           *MAM starts to cough. It stays with her till she sits
           down.*

MAUREEN   We're trying our best for you, Gerry. You do
          know that, don't you? Eee, talking of which... To
          go along with this... fresh start... I've got a
          proposition for you.

GERRY   I'm too young for you, Maureen, man. You
          wouldn't last past the wedding night.

MAUREEN   *(Smiles genuinely, then)* No, it's just a little
          trade, y'know? Like a swop, like. You do
          something for me... I've got something for *you*.
          Something I know you'd like.

GERRY   *(Recognizes that look in her eye)* Maureen, I'm
          not going to school... Purely no chance.

MAUREEN   No, listen to me, Gerry. If you go for, say, just
          two weeks...?

GERRY   Maureen man...

MAM   Gerry, listen to her, son.

GERRY   Mam, I'm *not* going to school. It's a hell-hole.
          You get taught nothing. All you get is treated like
          shite.

MAUREEN   *(Has heard this line before)* Well, according to
          you, you get that everywhere.

GERRY   Aye, mebbe, but I don't have to dress up like a
         prick to get it.

         *MUM shakes her head despondently. MAUREEN
         smiles determinedly.*

MAUREEN   You don't want to know what I've got for you if
          you go, then?

GERRY   No, cos I'm not going.

MAUREEN   I bet you do. In fact, I bet you're there today.

         GERRY shakes his head.

MAUREEN   (CONT.) Dressed up like a prick.

         She smiles, he doesn't.

MAUREEN   (CONT.) Two weeks, that's all you have to do.
          To get this ... certain something.

GERRY   I don't care what you've got, Maureen, watch me
         mouth: *I-am-not-going-to-school.* Not today or
         any other day. And there's nowt you could give
         me that'd make me change my mind, all right?

MAUREEN   Nowt?

GERRY   Totally. Nowt.

>Long pause as they stare at each other. Finally,
>MAUREEN sighs.

MAUREEN   Eeh, well I never. Gerry McCarten turning
down a pair of free tickets to the football.

>*Close-up of GERRY's reaction. Then CUT TO:*

36. INT. SCHOOL CLASSROOM. DAY.

>*A tight shot of GERRY, looking distinctly ill at
>ease in a school uniform. The camera pulls back
>to reveal him sitting at a desk among the rest of
>class 10/7. His form master, MR CAIRD, mid-
>forties, rests a buttock on his own desk in what
>he mistakenly believes is a cool pose. He
>alternates glances between GERRY and his own
>text of Shakespeare, which GERRY is reading
>out loud, not understanding a single bloody
>word, but nonetheless trying hard.*

GERRY   *'... Be innocent of the knowledge dearest...
chuck Till thou applaud the dead...'*

CAIRD   The deed.

GERRY   *'...the deed. Come, ceiling light...'*

CAIRD   Seeling *night*.

GERRY '*Come, seeling night, scarf up the tender eye of...*
       pitiful day, and with thy bloody invincible hand...'

CAIRD *(Sighs impatiently)* Bloody and invisible.

GERRY '*...Cancel and...tear to pieces that great bond...*
       which keeps me pale. Light chickens and the
       crow... makes wing...'

       The class begins to snigger.

CAIRD McCarten, don't push me, all right?

       Gerry looks up innocently.

CAIRD (CONT.) Or can you not read, lad? Maybe you're
       just lost without the pictures, eh?

       The class laughs, making CAIRD feel good.

CAIRD (CONT.) Janine, take over please. McCarten, you
       just stick to comics, eh?

JANINE '*Light thickens and the crow makes wing to the*
       rooky wood, Good things of day...'

       As JANINE resumes the text GERRY and CAIRD
       lock glares.

37. EXT. COUNCIL BUILDINGS. DAY.

RUSTY looks on in admiration as SEWELL digs over a large bed of soil in the square near the Council Offices. A PARK WORKER shovels a ton of daffodil bulbs out of the back of a truck, and shouts to SEWELL.

PARK WORKER   Where's the other lad, then?

SEWELL   Don't know.

PARK WORKER   Aye well, if you want the same money, you've still got to plant 'em all, reet?

SEWELL   Aye, reet.

SEWELL looks in dread at the mountain of bulbs.

38. INT. DINING ROOM. SCHOOL. DAY.

GERRY is in the dinner queue, waiting his turn for his alarmingly grey-looking lunch. His plate is handed from one dinner lady to another.

GERRY   No gravy, ta...

But the second DINNER LADY has already poured the clumpy brown matter on to his meal.

DINNER LADY   You what?

GERRY   No gravy. I don't want gravy.

DINNER LADY   You don't want gravy?

GERRY   I don't want gravy.

The DINNER LADY shakes her head in frustration, grabs a much-used dishcloth and uses it to wipe the gravy off the plate, then hands it over.

DINNER LADY   There you are.

GERRY   I'm not having that.

DINNER LADY   What's up *now*?

MR CAIRD and other TEACHERS, including a MISS WARREN, are on a nearby table.

CAIRD   McCarten, get a move on, you're holding things up.

GERRY   But did you see th...?

CAIRD   Don't argue, lad, just get on with it!

Shakes his head. To other teachers:

CAIRD   (CONT.) Bloody waste of space, that one.

          *We see MISS WARREN's obvious disapproval of
          CAIRD's technique. GERRY's bottom jaw juts out
          slightly in irritation as he glares back at CAIRD,
          who ignores him and salts his meal. As he
          continues to glare, we hear GERRY's voice
          overlapped:*

GERRY   (O/S) I don't know if I can stand it, Sewell man. I
          know it means we'll get to see the Toon, like, but
          I don't know… Caird's being a right old
          bastard…

39. EXT. MONUMENT. NEWCASTLE CITY CENTRE. DAY.

          *It's another day, a Saturday. GERRY, SEWELL
          and RUSTY sit by a hastily manufactured Guy
          Fawkes, a sign below it begging for Fifty Pennies
          for the Guy.*

SEWELL   It's only for a fortnight, Gerry man.

GERRY   I know, but I just want to chin him all the time.

SEWELL   Aye well. Chin him in a fortnight.

          *A disapproving WOMAN walks past. They see
          her shake her head.*

GERRY   What's up with you, like?

WOMAN   Why, it's only September, man.

GERRY   Aye, well, that's our motto, 'Be Prepared' like.

40. INT. ASSEMBLY ROOM. SCHOOL. DAY.

The uniformed class 10/7 are gathered in an uneven semicircle on the school stage in the assembly room, some sitting upright, some slumped on their sides with heads resting on elbow-supported hands, some lost in their own dreams, some glancing from time to time at their drama teacher, MISS WARREN, who is perched above them on a plastic stool. GERRY is included in two categories, being both slumped sideways and in his own dreams.

MISS WARREN   Come on, all of you, think... 'First times, first times'... Come on then, Gemma, the first time you...?

GEMMA   Did the Lottery, miss?

MISS WARREN   All right, the first time you did the Lottery? Describe what happened. And use similes. Remember what a simile is? When you say something is *like* something else.

GEMMA   It was like... well, it was like a disaster, miss.

MISS WARREN   A disaster?

GEMMA   We'd decided to use our birthdays as the numbers. You know, all six of our birthdays. Me dad went down the shop and did the ticket, like, and we all tuned in, like, and it started, you know, with that gadgie saying, 'Activate the Balls' and all that.

An uncontrollable snigger.

MISS WARREN   What's funny, Malcolm?

MALLY   Well, that wouldn't be a 'first time', miss. Gemma activating balls, like.

MISS WARREN   Yes, hilarious. Go on, Gemma.

GEMMA   Well, when the numbers come up, we'd won like.

JIMMY   Ha'way, I thought our stories had to be true.

GEMMA   It is true!

JIMMY   Lying coo.

MISS WARREN   Carry on, Gemma.

GEMMA   Anyway, all of us were jumping up and down, celebrating, like, going mad and that, like... Except for Dad, like.

MISS WARREN   Why not your dad?

GEMMA   Cos he'd... forgotten our birthdays miss. Got down shop and gone brain-dead, like. Forgotten our Dean's birthday. Forgotten my birthday. Forgotten *my mam's* birthday.

MISS WARREN   Oh dear... So... How did that feel? Use a simile. When you thought you'd won, and then realized your father had used different numbers. How did that feel? What did it feel *like*?

GERRY   Like a fucking great kick in the cunt I'd imagine.

MISS WARREN   Thank you, Gerry, we don't need *quite* such vivid comparisons.

GEMMA   Aye, but he's right, miss. Good similarity, that.

MISS WARREN   And what about your father? His perspective on the same experience must be very different to yours, yes?

MALLY   Nobody knows, miss, he's under the patio.

The class laughs.

MISS WARREN   Okay, okay... Now, anybody else. First times, first times...?

MALLY stretches up his hand, Miss Miss.

MISS WARREN   (CONT.) Thank you, Malcolm, but we've already had your all too graphic recollection of the morning after your first vindaloo...

GERRY is the only one without a hand up.

MISS WARREN   (CONT.) Gerry, what about you? You must have a first-time experience you can share with us?

He shakes his head.

MISS WARREN   (CONT.) Surely, all the things you get up to...?

Shakes his head again. MISS WARREN won't let him go so easily. She looks further into his eyes.

MISS WARREN   (CONT.) Come on Gerry, anything. What do you enjoy? What's your real passion?

GEMMA   Footie, miss, he's footie mad.

MISS WARREN   Ah yes, a regular member of the 'Toon Army', aren't you, Gerry?

MALLY   Not any more, miss, no one can get in now.

MISS WARREN   No, but you used to go, didn't you?

At last a reaction:

GERRY   *Course* I did, man.

MISS WARREN   What about the 'first time' you went to the football? I bet that was an experience. Why don't you tell us about that?

GERRY shakes his head.

MISS WARREN   (CONT.) Who took you? Your dad?

After a pause, GERRY finally nods.

GEMMA   Ha'way, Gerry man, tell us.

He receives various encouragement from the whole class and we see for the first time a shy side of GERRY. He looks up at MISS WARREN, who raises her eyebrows in kind encouragement too. All eyes are on Gerry. He finally stutters a start.

GERRY   I... I can't remember it that well, miss. It's that long ago, like. I was small... dead small, you know...

MISS WARREN   Try, Gerry.

GERRY   I was maybe five or six, can't remember exactly.
There was loads of people, people everywhere.
Dead noisy, but ... having a laugh, you know?
Well... we won, I think.

MISS WARREN   Go on. What else do you remember?

GERRY   My father's coat. I remember my father's coat. It
was dead thick and warm. Like a snorkel jacket,
you know? I was cold, you see, miss, so my
father gave me his jacket, and I put it on... right
round my face. I'd never been so warm. The
wind was whistling round the ground. It was
raining an'all. Didn't bother me though. I was
cushdy. And my father kept on looking down
from time to time to ask if I was all right. He was
shivering in a shirt and jumper, like, but he didn't
mind, as long as I was warm.

MISS WARREN   That was good of him.

GERRY   Aye. Then at half-time he bought us both a huge
steaming cup of tea. And we drank them
together.

MISS WARREN What was the tea *like*?

GERRY   Belter. Purely belter. Two sugars and *dead* milky, man. I don't know about similes, miss... it was just like... like... like the *best* cup of tea I've *ever* had. And after the whistle went we stayed put after everybody else'd gone. Then we walked through the park to get on a bus. It was the time of year when it's just getting dark about five, and I remember a bird singing in a tree, like. Don't know what sort... it was so long ago. Maybe one of them thrushes, miss. Whatever it was, it was singing *dead* loud. Just as it was getting dark, y'know? It was mint, man.

GERRY stares longingly into the middle-distance world of his own. There is now at last total silence in the room. MISS WARREN smiles.

MISS WARREN   And what about your father? His perspective on the same experience must be very different to yours, yes?

GERRY   Should think so. He's a fucking piss-head, miss.

There is a stunned beat before the whole class burst into laughter once more. Then immediately, the sudden sharp ringing of the end of lesson bell. There is instant mayhem as the class charge their exit. Slower to leave is GERRY. MISS WARREN shakes her head sadly as she watches him through the blur of hastily exiting uniform.

41. INT/EXT. ROAD INTO TOWN. DAY.

> *SEWELL is wearing a pair of cheap John Lennon
> sunglasses as black as the slightly too tight Toon
> Army baseball cap above them. He feel-taps at
> the pavement with a pool cue that has been
> recently (and somewhat unconvincingly) painted
> white. His other hand clutches a string, attached
> the end of which is a confused-looking RUSTY.
> These two and GERRY cut three very different
> figures as they walk in their various gaits towards
> the city.*

GERRY   We'll do C&A's, Smith's, Boots, Marks &
Sparks...

SEWELL   ...Everything's a Pound.

GERRY   *(Laughs)* Why aye, Everything's a Pound!

SEWELL   What's funny about that, like?

GERRY   Sewell man, we're going nicking. Nicking things
to sell. For proper money like.

SEWELL   Aye, I know that.

GERRY   Well, how much are we going to get for
something we nick from Everything's a Pound?

SEWELL   Well, depends what it's worth, like, dun't it.

GERRY   *Eh?* Well, what d'you *think* it'll be worth? Coming
         from a shop called Everything's a Pound?

SEWELL   Dunno, there's some good stuff in there.

GERRY   The most expensive thing in there, Sewell man,
         how much do you think that'll be, then?

         SEWELL chews it over.

GERRY   (CONT.) And, for that matter, the cheapest.

SEWELL   Jesus, one at a time man.

GERRY   It's the same bloody *question*, man.

SEWELL   *Eh?*

GERRY   Come on, then, tell us, eh?

         Pause.

         No need to panic, like. You've still got 50/50 and
         Phone a Friend. H'way, Sewell man, I'll give you
         a clue.The shop's called Everything's a
         Something.

SEWELL   I know what the bloody shop's *called*, man.

GERRY   Aye, well then, Everything's a Pound. Not Everything's a Tenner, or Everything's a Different Price. Everything's a Pound. So go on. How much is the dearest thing, *and* the cheapest thing? In a shop called Everything's a Pound?

SEWELL   Well, which do you want, man? The dearest or the cheapest?

GERRY   Both, man!

SEWELL   Eh?

GERRY   It's a fucking pound, man! Everything's a fucking pound!

SEWELL   Aye, I know, I know that! Jesus, man, I'm not stupid!

         They turn a corner and see the busy shopping streets. Theirs for the taking. Over this wide shot:

GERRY   All right, Einstein, so you're clear on the plan? While they're busy watching me, doing my decoy bit, pretending to nick, like, you just fill your pockets.

SEWELL   Aye, cos they won't see me cos I'm blind.

         GERRY sighs, patience tested.

GERRY   They'll *see* you, Sewell man, it's just they won't
         suspect you.

SEWELL   Why not?

GERRY   Cos you're *blind*, man! Cos you're *blind*!

SEWELL   Ah right, aye, I see.

         He sees GERRY's irritation.

SEWELL   (CONT.) Joke, Gerry man, it was a joke.

         SEWELL walks into a parked car.

42. INT. C&A. CITY CENTRE. DAY.

*We see their plan in action. GERRY waits for
security cameras to fix focus on him, then slides
clothing goods into a bag. We see the security
camera angle. He sees with satisfaction the
SECURITY man spring into walkie-talkie action.
More security people appear on the scene,
keeping their eye on GERRY, who continues
dropping items into his bag. Meanwhile,
SEWELL, unnoticed, is bagging shirts, ties, the
lot under his bench-coat. Finally, GERRY sees in
a mirror SEWELL and RUSTY leaving the store,
then makes to leave himself. Four SECURITY
men close in in preparation, but just before the*

*exit, he stops and empties the bag onto the floor,
smiles at them and leaves.*

43. INT. MARKS & SPENCERS FOOD HALL. CITY CENTRE. DAY.

*The same plan in Marks & Spencer's Food Hall,
except as each blood-raw packed rump steak
goes into SEWELL's coat, RUSTY's messy
waterfall of slaver is in real danger of attracting
attention. Finally as they leave, behind them in
the background we see a CUSTOMER slip and
fall on the wet floor.*

44. INT. BOOTS. CITY CENTRE. DAY.

*GERRY again attracting suspicion from
SECURITY. He looks across the store to SEWELL
and sighs. SEWELL is trying on a selection of
sunglasses, looking at himself in the mirror
provided. GERRY walks past him, hissing an angry
whisper out of the side of his mouth as he passes:*

GERRY   You're meant to be blind, you pillock man.

*SEWELL calmly takes the test pair off, revealing
eyes that are crossed, mainly white, and fixed
somewhere on the ceiling, and then puts his
Lennons calmly back on.*

45. INT. WATERSTONE'S. CITY CENTRE. DAY.

By the time they are in Waterstone's education section, SEWELL's bench-coat is bulging. He now looks like a blind bloke whose misfortune has been cruelly intensified by the additional disability of obesity. The same plan is in action once more, but GERRY sees a female ASSISTANT eyeing SEWELL with deep and, let's face it, understandable suspicion. SEWELL is beginning to sweat with what feels like coal bags in his coat. GERRY's sudden appearance at his elbow makes SEWELL jump.

GERRY   After you, sir!

Then whispers:

GERRY   (CONT.) *They're on to you.*

SEWELL heads nervously but determinedly for the door. On the way, in a vain attempt to fend off suspicion, he coolly browses the shelves as he goes. He's within reach of the exit when suddenly:

ASSISTANT   Can I help you?

SEWELL nearly turns to answer, but remembers his blindness. Instead, he looks in completely the wrong direction. He's chuffed with his cunning.

SEWELL   No thanks, just browsing.

ASSISTANT   That's an unusual guide dog. Where was he
          trained?

SEWELL   Em... In Whickham.

ASSISTANT   Ah, I know Whickham. Whereabouts?

SEWELL   Em... In the woods up there... y'know...

ASSISTANT   Woods?

SEWELL   ...Aye... and... all them... fields round about.

ASSISTANT   Strange.

> SEWELL's throat fills. He tries to clear it. He
> finally plucks up courage and turns to face her.
> He sees behind her GERRY's attempts to deflect
> attention, putting textbooks openly and with
> great exaggeration into his bag. He might as well
> be shouting out, 'Look at me, I am stealing!' But
> nobody is paying any attention.

SEWELL   Why's that, like?

ASSISTANT   Well, you know, they usually train guide dogs
          in towns and cities, on streets, where people *live*.

SEWELL   Not this one, cos... I live in... a field, like.

ASSISTANT   You live in a field?

SEWELL   Aha. And woods, like. Woods. Trees, y'know. Out
in the wilds like.

ASSISTANT   Whereabouts?

*It's hot in Waterstones, and for SEWELL, laden
with a ton of tutelage, getting hotter all the time.
He feels like a piece of bacon spitting under the
grill. It is quite evident that, somewhere under
that bench-coat, a major panic is building. In the
distance behind her, GERRY is still openly
bagging books.*

SEWELL   You wouldn't know it... I live ... miles from
anywhere. With ponies and huskies, them
Newfoundland dogs an'all, with the webbed feet,
y'know...? Snows most of the year... Big castles.

*This torrent of nonsense gets the pause it
deserves.*

ASSISTANT   Browsing, you say?

SEWELL   Aye, just browsing.

ASSISTANT   Just browsing?

SEWELL   You're not deaf, are you?

ASSISTANT   No, I'm not deaf. And you're not blind.

> Finally SEWELL opens his eyes. He looks directly
> at the ASSISTANT. Her face is hard and cold.
> SEWELL looks round for GERRY, who is now
> walking out of the shop with books held high,
> still nobody paying him, ironically, a blind bit of
> notice. The ASSISTANT finally turns and sees
> him. She looks back to SEWELL but he has
> disappeared already. The ASSISTANT runs out
> after him but as she gets to the door, RUSTY
> suddenly reappears in the doorway, blocking her
> exit by growling as nastily as his good nature will
> allow. She's a sensible woman – those teeth look
> sharp and, what the hell, they're not her books
> anyway. She returns into the shop. We hear,
> overlapped, the blood-curdling din that is
> Metroland. It sounds like a slaughterhouse, or at
> the very least the scene of a very ugly
> massacre...

46. INT. METROLAND FUNFAIR – METRO CENTRE. DAY.

> Metroland is an enormous indoor amusement
> park within the Metro Shopping Centre. It is big
> enough to contain roller-coaster rides, the lot, a
> mass of garish jingling colour and light. There is
> also a rail track for a kiddies' train, which moves
> slowly past shoppers, over level-crossings etc.

GERRY rushes in, breathless and obviously looking for SEWELL, but he sees no sign of him. Among the cacophony of sound he thinks he hears his name shouted. He turns but sees nothing. And again. And then again:

SEWELL (O/S) Gerry!! Ha'way man Gerry!! It's belter! Geeeerrrryyyy!!!

GERRY finally spots SEWELL, who, clutching RUSTY by his side, sits in a cab on the massive overhead roller-coaster ride. GERRY yells at him as he roars past:

GERRY Sewell, man, you're meant to be blind, man!!

SEWELL *(Swishes into the distance)* Aye! We're allowed to have fun an'all, y'know!!

47. INT. CARRIAGE. BALLOON WHEEL. METROLAND FUNFAIR. DAY.

In the carriage of a balloon wheel ride, we find GERRY and SEWELL and squeezed between them, watching the world go by, RUSTY. SEWELL is itemizing and transferring the booty from his coat into a big bag, while GERRY still keeps a lookout for any pursuant security men.

SEWELL   ...Three ladies' shirts, two skirts... some bras
          and knickers, a scarf... two pairs of gloves... a
          rubber duck and...

GERRY   Eh?

SEWELL   Three ladies' shirts...

GERRY   A rubber duck?

SEWELL   For little Sheara, like. Bathtime, y'know.

GERRY   And what's that there?

SEWELL   Ah, that's just, you know, sort of body spray
          stuff. I just... it's just a present, like.

GERRY   Who for?

SEWELL   Nobody.

GERRY   Nobody? Aye well, nobody's gonna love that.
          Anyway, no, I meant this, you greedy bastard.

          *GERRY pulls out of the coat an empty plastic
          sandwich package.*

SEWELL   Ha'way, Marks's Chicken Tikka, man. I cannot
          resist them, Gerry man.

Suddenly and without warning GERRY frantically digs out the textbooks from his own bag and plunges the empty bag over RUSTY's head. RUSTY yelps the dog equivalent of 'What the fuck...?'

SEWELL   Jesus man, what are you doing?

GERRY   Act natural.

SEWELL   Eh?

Then SEWELL sees what GERRY obviously saw. Lingering at the foot of the ride, sticking out like a sore thumb among the toddlers and Mums, is MATTHEW BRABIN. His neck and head twitch in a convulsive movement, like a starved alligator trying to get off a leash. He chews gum, possibly his own, with ferocious passion. His eyes dart around the whole area, scouring as if it's become second nature, as if he's been scouring so long it's become a habit. SEWELL hasn't got time to do anything but put his sunglasses back on and sit bolt upright, like GERRY, and look straight ahead. We see them pass right behind MATTHEW, who gives them a look, then a second look, but no more. When the balloon rises again, MATTHEW crosses and goes into the distance.

48. INT. CORRIDOR. SCHOOL. DAY.

GERRY, bulging carrier bag in hand, approaches a BOY and GIRL waiting outside a classroom.

GERRY   Hey, you're top set, aren't you?

They both nod.

GERRY   (CONT.) Do you want to buy some books?

GIRL   No, thanks.

GERRY   Ha'way, look at them first, man.

He takes a book out of the bag.

GERRY   (CONT.) Now that's beautiful, just what you need, man.

GIRL   We don't do Spanish here.

GERRY   So?

GIRL   So... Why would I want a Spanish dictionary?

GERRY   Well, I don't know, hinny, you might want to go to Spain on your holidays, like. How are you going to shag the Diego lads if you don't know the lingo, like?

She looks at him disapprovingly.

GERRY   (CONT.) How's about this then? A hardback, like.
         A classic. See, it says *'Everyman's Classic. A
         Sportsman's Notebook'*.

BOY   What's it about?

GERRY   Footie. Keegan wrote it before he left the Toon.

BOY   It says, *'by Ivan Turgenev'*.

GERRY   Well aye, he helped him, like. Couldn't do
         everything on his own, you know, our Kev. Ivan
         helped him out like. You know Ivan Turkeyoff?
         Canny player, looked like a fish but.

BOY   How much?

GERRY   About eight hundred thou, I think. From Dynamo
         Kiev.

BOY   For the book.

         *CAIRD, dressed in a flashy tracksuit, appears at
         the doors at the end of the corridor. He sees
         GERRY.*

CAIRD   McCarten, what are you playing at?! You're
         meant to be changed and in the gym, lad!

GERRY   I've got no decent kit.

CAIRD   I've got no decent kit, *sir*.

GERRY   Aye, well, that makes two of us then.

          CAIRD glares, as far from amused as is possible.
          CUT TO:

49. INT. SCHOOL GYM. DAY.

          We see a game of bench football taking place in
          the gym, but it is upside-down. Eventually, into
          an upside-down close-up, walks CAIRD. He
          leans into the camera. Talks quietly, nastily:

CAIRD   You see, McCarten, there's kids here, good kids,
          who come in every day for years and years and
          sometimes go out the far end with nothing. You
          turn up for a fortnight, and what do you get? A
          bloody present. Aye, I've heard all about it. All
          these kids, you see, they come here to get
          educated. But you, you come here to get...
          football tickets. And you know what that makes
          me feel, McCarten? Fucking sick, that's what.
          And there's only one thing I can do to make me
          feel better. And that's to make that fucking
          fortnight a fucking *misery* for you. Stay up there
          till the bell.

Gerry (CHRIS BEATTIE) and
Sewell (GREG McLANE) on the run.

Mam (CHARLIE HARDWICK) and
Clare (TRACY WHITWELL) at the bingo.

Sewell and Gemma (JODY BALDWIN).

Gerry and Sewell caught in the act.

Sewell has a quiet word with Rusty (BEN).

Sewell and Gerry.

Sewell and Gerry on the scrounge.

Sewell pretends to be blind.

Sewell, Gerry and the ever-faithful Rusty.

The Angel of the North.

Gerry and Sewell confront their hero.

Gerry and Sewell push their trolley looking for rag and bone.

Gerry and Sewell with their mates.

Mark Herman on set.

We cut wide, and back the right way up, to see
GERRY hanging upside down, puce-faced, from
*the wall bars. CUT TO **BLACK**.*

50. EXT. SUBURBAN STREET. NIGHT.

In the dark we can just make out GERRY and
SEWELL. The camera precedes them as they jog
along the pavement, eyes closed, singing in
strangely quiet tones:

GERRY AND SEWELL   *'Ah, me lads, ye shoulda seen us*
                gannin,
                Passin the folks along the road Just as they were
                stannin'
                Aal the lads an' lasses there aal wi smilin faces...
                Gannin alang the Scotswood Rooooooad
                T'see the... Blaydon Races.'

They skid to a halt outside a house, but GERRY
moves on towards a house further up the street.

SEWELL   Where are you going, Gerry man? This is it. The
        house at the end of the song. We always do the
        house at the end of the song.

GERRY   Not tonight, Sewell man.

51. INT. DOWNSTAIRS. SUBURBAN HOUSE. NIGHT.

The BLACK is broken by the beams of two torch-beams dancing on a frosted window. We see the shapes of the two ski-hatted heads, one much higher than the other. We hear the noise of a forced window.

52. INT. UPSTAIRS BEDROOM. SUBURBAN HOUSE. NIGHT.

GERRY's torch-beam frantically follows every item he takes off a surface and into his heavy-duty-bin liner. From elsewhere in the house we still hear the humming of 'Blaydon Races'.

GERRY   *Whssht*, stop that humming man!

SEWELL   (O/S) I can't help it, man Gerry. Whenever I'm buzzing I start humming.

GERRY   Cut it out, man. Ha'way look, a vid in the bedroom. They're well loaded.

53. INT. BATHROOM. SUBURBAN HOUSE. NIGHT.

SEWELL picks up a spray.

SEWELL   Hey, look at this tackle.

> *He sprays under his bench-coat, shines a light at it.*

SEWELL   (CONT.) Lily of the Valley. The lasses'll be all over us with this gear.

> *GERRY, heaving the bin-liner, appears in the doorway.*

GERRY   It's air-freshener, man. You don't spray air freshener on.

SEWELL   Aye, you can.

GERRY   No, you can't. It's for when you've been, man. To clear the air like.

SEWELL   'Been'? What are you on about?

GERRY   You spray it all around after you've had a shite. If you go about with that gear on, all the lasses'll think you've just had a shite.

> *He sees SEWELL pocketing the air-freshener.*

GERRY   (CONT.) Put it back, man, you don't break into a house to nick air-freshener.

SEWELL You do if you live with *my* dad. You'd reckon this stuff was gold dust.

GERRY All right, take it, man Sewell, but no more junk, eh? Ha'way, let's go downstairs.

SEWELL pockets the air-freshener, tapping it tenderly.

SEWELL Pure gold dust.

54. INT. KITCHEN. SUBURBAN HOUSE. NIGHT.

Their swag bag weighs a ton now as we find them in the kitchen. A fridge hums in a corner. Units are at eye level, carved from gleaming wood. Pots and pans hang from rings screwed into the walls. SEWELL opens a dishwasher.

SEWELL Jesus, they don't even have to wash their own dishes, they just stick them in here, look. An' look, a coffee-maker, a toaster, a microwave... Can't these bastards do anything for themselves?

GERRY Ha'way, we'll have the microwave... and something for our dinner.

He takes a roast chicken from the fridge and puts it inside the microwave.

GERRY   (CONT.) Ha'way Sewell, it's time we was missing.

As they unplug the microwave, SEWELL begins humming 'Blaydon Races' again. Carrying the microwave, SEWELL follows GERRY across the kitchen towards the hall. GERRY grabs a pot storage jar from a surface as he passes. He tips all the rice out onto the floor.

GERRY   (CONT.) That'll do for our money tin.

Suddenly the front door opens and the hall light goes on. GERRY and SEWELL freeze, instinctively stooping, making themselves smaller. A large voice fills the hall.

DENISE   You always say 'never again', but we always end up going. Whenever her ladyship calls.

MAN   Oh, not that again, pet.

SEWELL recognizes the voice and, wide-eyed, turns to GERRY, who nods, and smiles. We see their POV. It is Mr and Mrs CAIRD.

DENISE   Yes, that again. I'm not saying you fancy her, Paul man, I mean who'd fancy an old tart with her tongue and tits hanging out like that. You'd have to be a real saddo to fancy *her*.

CAIRD   Denise... I don't fancy her...

DENISE   Aye well, for someone who *doesn't* fancy her you
          spend a load of time looking at her tits.

CAIRD   I wasn't looking at her tits.

DENISE   Drooling like a lunatic, you were.

GERRY   *(Whispers)* I bet he was an'all. Ha'way, man
          Sewell, let's get missing.

CAIRD   I don't look at other women, pet. Why should I?
          When me wife's got the top tits on Tyneside?

          SEWELL and GERRY lurch into silent giggles.
          The CAIRDS wander through into the darkness
          of the living room.

DENISE   (O/S) Honest?

CAIRD   (O/S) Uh huh.

DENISE   (O/S) Are you going to tell *them* that?

CAIRD   (O/S) Go on then.

          We hear CAIRD's voice, usually one of authority
          and discipline at school, now reduced to childish
          gibberish as he munches cleavage. GERRY and
          SEWELL look in severe pain as they desperately
          try to keep their hysterical laughter silent.
          SEWELL covers his mouth but that doesn't stop

a noise coming out the other end, a high-pitched fart echoing through the hallway. The slurping in the living room suddenly stops. The whole world seems to stop.

DENISE   (O/S) What the hell was *that*?

We hear the room light switch on. It lights up our heroes.

GERRY   *Run for it!*

GERRY hurriedly opens and makes to scamper out of the back door, but the bin-liner is too widely packed for the door-frame. He tries to heave it through but can't.

GERRY   (CONT.) Agh *fuck it!!*

He reluctantly drops the bin-liner and carries on out. SEWELL, in his speedy effort to follow, and with the microwave he is carrying creating a major blind-spot, skids on the rice. He just manages to steady himself, only to then trip over the dumped bin-bag and hurtle horizontally into the back garden.

54A. EXT. REAR GARDEN. SUBURBAN HOUSE. NIGHT.

> *The microwave hits the path just before he does. Its door springs open and the chicken flies out, skidding along the path and into the flower bed. Cursing, SEWELL picks himself and the microwave up.*

GERRY   Run, man! She's at the frigging door!

> *SEWELL turns back to see the thick-set squat figure of DENISE CAIRD standing in the doorway, blouse buttons undone.*

DENISE   Paul! *Paul?!*

55. INT. LIVING ROOM. SUBURBAN HOUSE. NIGHT.

> *But CAIRD is still in the living room, his hand still on the light switch, his eyes on the living room wallpaper, freshly enhanced with a spray-painted message, which he has to tilt his head to read:*

DENISE   (O/S) Paul, where are you!?

56. EXT. REAR GARDEN. SUBURBAN HOUSE. NIGHT.

> *Back in the garden, SEWELL is still paralysed, rooted to the spot. He can hear GERRY shouting but can't move.*

GERRY   Run, man!!

WOMAN   Come here you bastards! Paul!

GERRY   Cover your face, man!

> *SEWELL is like a rabbit caught in the headlights. Finally, he drops the microwave, pulls his Toon ski-hat down over his face, turns and promptly runs smack bang into a tree. CAIRD comes to the door as GERRY returns to pick SEWELL up and guide him at speed out into the darkness. All they have with them as they run down the street is the single empty pot jar.*

> *SLOW FADE to BLACK.*

57. EXT. MCCARTEN BUNGALOW (2). DAY.

> *FADE UP as SEWELL walks, shoulders slumped, sulkily, towards Gerry's front door. RUSTY, in his gloomy trail, seems to have a cob on too. He bangs twice, hard, on the door. GERRY*

immediately comes out. He too is well wrapped up. He too seems miserable, and not a word is spoken as he joins them and the three march back up the street in bolshy union. CUT TO:

58. EXT. BUS STATION. DAY.

Their bottom lips almost on the ground, SEWELL, RUSTY and GERRY stand in a silent line at the bus stop. We can almost see a black cloud over their heads. CUT TO:

59. INT. BUS. DAY.

On the bus, RUSTY is squeezed between GERRY and SEWELL. They all look in different directions. The CONDUCTOR comes round and prompts the first words of the day.

GERRY   Two and a dog to the football ground.

The CONDUCTOR takes their money and leaves them to another long simmering silence. Finally

GERRY   (CONT.) Ha'way, Sewell, I got them for free, didn't I?

No reaction.

GERRY   (CONT.) I was *conned*, man. How was I meant to
             know, eh?

SEWELL   *I* don't know, do I? You're the brains. Agh, I can't
             believe it, man.

GERRY   She knows nothing about football, Maureen, the
             old trout. 'Couple of free tickets,' she said. She
             didn't say where for.

SEWELL   I can't believe it.. I just can't believe... We're
             going to see *Sunderland*!

             Even RUSTY nearly shakes his head in shame.

GERRY   Sewell man... We're not going to *see* them! We're
             going there to sell our tickets. Get good money
             for these an'all. All towards tickets we frigging
             want.

60. EXT. STREET NR STADIUM OF LIGHT. SUNDERLAND. DAY.

*There are crowds of people in a busy street near
the ground. The excited buzz of match day.
GERRY, SEWELL and RUSTY turn a corner into
the street. Then GERRY suddenly stops. He puts
an arm out to stop SEWELL too. RUSTY comes
to a halt of his own accord. They all gaze
towards the end of the street.*

GERRY   Ha'way, Sewell, look, man. The Stadium of Light.

*We see their POV. Rising like a space station
above the terrace houses: The enormous
Stadium of Light. Home of Sunderland AFC. It is
magnificent.*

SEWELL   Stadium o'Shite, you mean.

*One of a large group of lads glances at Sewell as
they pass by. GERRY grabs SEWELL by the coat
and drags him along the rest of the street,
talking in hushed tones.*

GERRY   Sewell, man, are you kamikaze or what? We're in
the heart of enemy territory now. Don't talk from
now on. Not a word.

SEWELL   Eh? Man alive, man.

GERRY   See? You speak pure Geordie. Open your mouth
like that round here and you're dead meat.
They'll rip you to shreds, man, and afterwards all
we'll find of you is a few scraps of your bench-
coat blowing along Roker beach. All right?

*SEWELL thinks about answering but, worried by
the warning, decides it's safer just to nod. They
have arrived now at the concourse of the
stadium. Big crowds, programme sellers, hot
dogs, noise. They are the only figures standing*

still, sticking out like three sore thumbs. They
look around, intrigued by and slightly in awe of
the surrounding excitement.

GERRY   (CONT.) Ha'way, man, why don't we just go in
         and watch?

SEWELL   *Eh?* Watch *Sunderland*?

GERRY   We're not going to sell our tickets now, are we?
         They've all got them.

SEWELL   Watch... *Sunderland*?

         An enormous roar fills the air. Obviously
         Sunderland have just run out. It is a sound they
         can't ignore. Nor indeed resist. The camera
         closes in on them as they stare up at the
         stadium.

SEWELL   (CONT.) I s'ppose... we've nothing better to do,
         like. Stay, Rusty, we'll be back, quarter to five.

GERRY   Dogs can't tell the time, man.

61. INT. STAIRCASE. STADIUM OF LIGHT. DAY.

         The famed 'Roker Roar' has moved along with
         the club to this spanking new stadium. It builds
         and builds to a crescendo as SEWELL and

GERRY come in through the turnstiles and run
up the stairs. Except it isn't just up the stairs, it's
up and up and up and up the stairs. They are
breathless when they reach the top, where the
camera follows them through the entrance. They
may not be quite on top of the world but it feels
like it. Seemingly miles below, the game has just
kicked off. So far down, it looks like it is being
played by Subbuteo teams. The two lads sway
momentarily with vertigo. The camera again
closes in on them. They are obviously overawed
but reluctant to show it. We hear the Sunderland
fans singing:

CROWD   'Fuck 'em all, fuck 'em all,
Shearer, Shepherd and Hall.
We'll never be mastered
by Black & White bastards
Cos Sund'lund's best of 'em all.'

GERRY   Not bad.

SEWELL   Not a patch on St James's, like, but aye, so-so.

62. INT./EXT. STADIUM OF LIGHT. DAY.

GERRY and SEWELL sit tight in their seats
looking down over a sea of red and white to the
pitch, where the massive oohs and aahs tell us
an exciting encounter is taking place. They are

enjoying hot polystyrene cups of tea. A chant so
loud they can't ignore:

CROWD   *'If ye hate Newcastle clap yer hands,*
If ye hate Newcastle clap yer hands,
If ye hate Newcastle, hate Newcastle,
Hate Newcastle clap yer hands.'

Everyone around them joins in clapping. GERRY
and SEWELL have to suffer the indignity of
joining in too. Regardless of this, we can see in
their eyes that this is a massive experience. They
are like innocent children again. Sunderland
push forward. The crowd's huge tuneful unison
gets louder.

CROWD   (CONT.) *'Cheer up, Peter Reid,*
Oh what can it mean...' (etc.)

GERRY   This is it, Sewell, my old mate. Next season,
this'll be us at St James's. Maybe we'll have a
couple of seats like this. Course, the football'll
be much better like, but you still get a sense of it
here. Sewell, I counted the jar again this
morning. We're almost there, son, we're almost
there.

CROWD   *'Wise men say, only fools rush in,*
But ah can't help falling in love with ye.'

GERRY   Ha'way, Sewell. Tell us that thing again.

SEWELL   What thing?

GERRY   Y'know man. About the time your dad took you to St James's.

SEWELL   Oh that. Why, man?

GERRY   No reason. I just like it, that's all.

SEWELL   *(Sips his tea, blows away the steam)* Well, it was years ago. In them days anyone could go. You didn't have to be loaded. You just paid at the gate. Stood anywhere you wanted. Was dead cold, brass monkeys, I remember that. And I remember... my dad gave me his coat. Even though it meant that he was cold. He kept on looking down to see if I was okay. He was freezing his bollocks off in a jumper, like, but he didn't mind, as long as I was warm.

The camera closes in on the listener rather than the narrator. Obviously, we have heard this story before. We see in GERRY's eyes not jealousy or envy, more just a plain and simple sadness.

SEWELL   (CONT.) At half-time he bought us a cup of hot tea. Two sugars and *dead* milky, man. Better than this one, y'know, different class. It was the best cup of tea I've ever had. Afterwards we stayed put for a while. Stood in the empty ground, like, just me and him. We were in no hurry. Then we walked through the park and there was this bird singing in a tree, like. Dead loud. I remember that. Then we went home. That was it.

GERRY   Was it the best day of your life?

SEWELL   *(Thinks a moment)* I don't know yet, do I?

          GERRY smiles. Then a long pause before he braves it:

GERRY   Sewell, man?

SEWELL   Aye?

GERRY   This is me first football match. I've never been before. Never even seen the Toon play, me.

          SEWELL turns to face him, looks at him a while, then:

SEWELL   I know *that*, you dozy cunt.

          The moment is interrupted by the eruption of a Sunderland goal. Everyone around them jumps to their feet. SEWELL grabs the back of GERRY's neck and shakes it fondly. SLOW FADE.

63. INT. MCCARTEN BUNGALOW (2). NIGHT.

GERRY enters and turns on the light, surprised that it's off in the first place.

GERRY   Mam?

He wanders to the kitchen area and sees a piece of paper on top of a pile of white curly corned-beef sandwiches. He smiles. The paper reads: 'Gerry, gone to Bingo, back 11.00. Mam.' His smile drops when he hears a shuffling noise from the bedroom end of the house. He stands rooted to the spot for a shocked moment, then, finally, plucks up courage to creep nervously towards it. On the balls of his feet, he edges across the living room, where he hears it again, another shuffle of paper. It is coming from BRIDGET's room. Palms sweating, he slowly pushes open the door:

GERRY   Bridget...?

64. INT. BRIDGET'S ROOM. MCCARTEN BUNGALOW (2). NIGHT.

He flicks the light switch but the light doesn't come on. It takes him a moment to become accustomed to the darkness, but he can see a vague figure hunched on the bed...

GERRY   Ha'way, Bridge? I know it's you, sis.

The silence and darkness are punctured by the crack and flare of a match from the bed in the corner, and a puff of smoke as it's applied to a cigarette. The lips turn a gaudy red by the match flame, which is then waved out. Then the mouth speaks:

VOICE   All right, Gerry?

GERRY freezes. Like ice.

VOICE   (CONT.) Come in, son, and say hello to your old man, eh?

With that the bedside lamp is clicked on and we see him, Gerry's DAD, unshaven, eyes droopy-lidded, and slightly akimbo. We can almost smell the booze, his bloated belly testing the seams of his grubby shirt. Gerry would have preferred the light to stay off, because he likes nothing that he sees. His DAD and, beside him on the bed, Bridget's private shoebox, opened, its contents scattered on the mattress: a comic, magazines, school exercise books, a hairbrush, various pictures of Bridget at various ages. He is holding the most recent one. GERRY's eyes wander to the corner, where the cupboard door is open, its contents all over the floor, and there, in the middle of the room, the pot storage jar. Empty. GERRY's hands clench into fists.

GERRY   You b... Those are hers... And that was mine...

DAD   Oh, grow up, son. B'sides, all them years I fed
         and clothed you. All them times I helped you out.
         You fuckin' owe it me.

GERRY   You cannet do this...

DAD   Oh aye? You gonna stop me, eh? Agh, don't be a
         prick all your life, son. You're no bigger now than
         last time I decked ye. How's your mam?

         GERRY refuses to answer

DAD   (CONT.) I still love her, you know that?

GERRY   Aye, I saw her lip, last time you came. Must have
         been some fucking kiss, that.

DAD   And you might not like this, Gerry son, but she
         still loves me.

         GERRY laughs dismissively.

DAD   (CONT.) She does. I can tell. And you know
         what? We'll all be back together again, sooner
         than you know it, son. Back like before.

         He looks down again at one of the photos.

DAD   (CONT.) Where's Bridge?

GERRY   How did you find us?

          *DAD begins to laugh an ugly, beery, Woodbine
          laugh.*

DAD   That's what I mean. You'll never guess, go on...
          you'll never guess.

          It's obvious GERRY isn't going to try.

DAD   (CONT.) What do I do, Gerry son? What's my job,
          man?

          GERRY's heart sinks.

DAD   (CONT.) The bins, man!

          DAD laughs more than it warrants.

DAD   (CONT.) You've moved to my patch, you pillocks!
          How fucking easy can she make it?! She *must*
          want me back!

          The laugh cuts deep at GERRY.

GERRY   *You bastard, you...!*

          *He marches swiftly towards his DAD, on the way
          picking up the storage jar and adjusting it in his
          hand for premium force and, all in the same
          motion, raising it high above his head. In the split*

second before it comes down, DAD flashes out a
lightning fist at GERRY's chin. GERRY seems to
fall in slow motion. The storage jar smashes
against the wall and lands in pieces on the floor
even before GERRY does, lights well and truly out.

SLOW FADE TO BLACK.

65. INT. TOILET. MCCARTEN FLAT. (3) SCOULER HILL. DAY.

GERRY is having a crap. He's shivering and
looks blue with cold. He hears a long, drawn-out
'ssshh' noise and is confused because he is
convinced that it is not coming from his
anatomy. He looks down between his legs to
check. No. The noise gets slightly louder. He
looks up and sees a roll of damp wallpaper
unfurling itself from the ceiling – 'ssshhh'. A title:

'Winter'

66. INT. SEWELL FLAT. DUNSTON ROCKET. DAY.

Christmas meal in the SEWELL household. MR
SEWELL is still pottering in the kitchen as
SEWELL brings a small turkey to the table. Both
SEWELL and MR SEWELL have Christmas
cracker hats on to add Yuletide cheer to the

surroundings. SEWELL is about to start carving but notices the black stuffing dribbling out of the turkey's rear end. He frowns at its deep hue. He prods it, pokes a bit more of it out, and it tumbles onto the plate. He frowns again. Very tentatively he dips his finger in it, more tentatively brings it to his nose, and even more tentatively still decides to taste it.

MR SEWELL   What's up, son? What have I done now?

SEWELL can hardly bring himself to break the news.

SEWELL   You've put... Christmas pud... in the... No matter, eh? Saves time, like. All ends up in the bog together, doesn't it?

MR SEWELL looks at SEWELL with a look that breaks your heart. SEWELL starts carving.

67. EXT. MCCARTEN FLAT. (3) SCOULER HILL. NIGHT.

GERRY was right, they are getting smaller. And crappier. In comparison to this, Craggs Estate was Mayfair. The blue sky of winter night surrounds the huge tatty block of council flats. But at one window a golden Christmas warmth seems to shine from the window out onto the

tiny balcony, the floor of which is home to the
now sad and scraggy-looking square of turf.

68. INT. MCCARTEN FLAT. (3). SCOULER HILL. NIGHT

Not so Christmassy once you're inside. The door
has an inordinate amount of locks and bolts on
it. CLARE is changing SHEARA's nappy in the
middle of the small main room. MAM looks tired
and ill. She coughs heavy and long. GERRY is
unpacking one of several removals boxes. There
are still the remains of a scabby bruise on his
chin. MAUREEN is there too, hanging some
cheap decorations in a futile attempt to add a bit
of festive atmosphere. Even her fixed smile is
beginning to tire. MAM finally finishes coughing
and spits a blob of phlegm into a piece of toilet
paper. At her elbow there is a toilet roll and
about twenty rolled-up pieces. John and Yoko's
'War is Over' plays on a radio.

MAM   *'Lets hope it's a good one',* eh, Maureen?

MAUREEN   Absolutely.

MAM   *'Without any fear.'* Be an angel, Gerry pet, shut
          them curtains.

          GERRY goes to close the curtains.

MAUREEN   And that's what you're saying? You fell down
           the stairs?

           GERRY glances at his MAM, who glances back.
           Reluctantly:

GERRY   Aye.

MAUREEN   It's hard to buy that one.

GERRY   Why's that, like?

MAUREEN   Well... what with it being a bungalow, like...? I
           don't understand... You could get him this time.
           Get a Court Order on him.

GERRY   It's not a Court Order he wants, it's Last Rites.

MAUREEN   Aye well, I don't think we can arrange *that*.

GERRY   Never know with you lot. Y'managed to mix up
         N'castle and Sunderland. You could manage
         anything.

69. EXT. BARRETT ESTATE. NEWCASTLE. NIGHT.

           GERRY, SEWELL and RUSTY stand, well
           wrapped in the cold, outside their umpteenth
           house, hurriedly finishing off:

111

GERRY AND SEWELL   '...sle-eep in heavenly pee-eace.
Jingle bells jingle bells, jingle all the way,
Oh what fun it is to see
the Geordies win away, hey...'

The door opens and a GRANNY type offers them
each a boiled sweet.

SEWELL   Sweets? I'm seventeen, man!

OLD DEAR   Merry Christmas, lads.

SEWELL   Aye, and a Happy New Hearing Aid.

OLD DEAR   Ta, son, same to you.

The door closes on them. SEWELL looks at his
watch.

SEWELL   Ha'way, I'm off, man.

GERRY   Where to?

SEWELL   Out and about, like, you know.

He nods at GERRY's bag of change.

SEWELL   (CONT.) We've done all right, yeah? We've got to
be nearly there now, eh?

GERRY   *(Can't bring himself to tell him)* Aye, aye, nearly
          there.

SEWELL   See you, then.

GERRY   *(Plucks up courage)* Sewell man...?

SEWELL   Aye?

GERRY   Nothing. See you.

70. EXT. BOATYARD. NIGHT.

*It is snowing now. The camera tracks through
moored boats and finds one boat, on land. We
see a glimmer from within.*

70A. INT. BOAT. NIGHT.

SEWELL   Aye, I know it's not the Ritz but. Anywhere's
          cushdy with you there. Just... belter... to have a
          place to ourselves. Just you and me, y'know?

          *We see the object of his dialogue. GEMMA is
          alongside him on the seat. She has not exactly
          dressed to battle the elements, a boob tube and
          a skirt that's as short as it is tight hardly fending
          off the cold.*

GEMMA   Aye, just you and me... and Rusty.

We see RUSTY across the cabin, staring at them, slavering.

SEWELL   Rusty'll be no bother, man.

GEMMA   Hey, you know that mad kid I told you about? The one looking for his dog? Apparently he's asking around, like. Looking everywhere. He's off his heed that lad.

SEWELL   Aye, well, so'd I be if someone nicked me hound.

GEMMA   I don't think it was nicked. He just lost it, like.

SEWELL   Oh... Aye. Like you've lost that Zak felluh, aye?

GEMMA   Aye. Like that.

SEWELL   You have lost him, Gemma, haven't you?

GEMMA   Aye, he's gone for good has Zak. History. Can't be doing with tossers, me.

SEWELL   Gissa kiss then, eh, Gemma?

She looks at him and smiles. Leans into him and virtually opens his mouth with her tongue. When she pulls away he looks like he's run a marathon.

SEWELL   Jesus.

GEMMA   What?

SEWELL   Nothing. Hey, I've got you a Christmas present.

GEMMA   Aah, Sewell, you needn't have.

SEWELL   It's only small, like.

He glances down to his flies.

SEWELL   (CONT.) ...but it's gettin' bigger all the time.

She laughs a dirty laugh and climbs on to him, a knee either side of his hips. They lunge into each other's throats again. They come up for breath. GEMMA looks down, and starts unzipping his trousers. We cut to a wide shot, the boat, the boatyard. Snowflakes fall as passions rise.

GEMMA   Hey, you know... A cock's not just for Christmas, it's for life.

SEWELL   I wouldn't mind that, Gemma pet.

GEMMA   Ha'way then, Sewell man, are you going to get out of that bench-coat?

SEWELL   Not if I needn't, no.

FADE.

71. INT. METRO TRAIN. DAY.

FADE UP: On SEWELL's happy face. The Metro train rattles out of a tunnel and towards the coast. SEWELL, whistling chirpily, and RUSTY sit on a seat opposite GERRY, whose forehead vibrates on the window.

71A. EXT. TYNEMOUTH STATION. DAY.

SEWELL is the dreaded life and soul as he, GERRY and RUSTY cross the bridge in Tynemouth railway station.

SEWELL   Ha'way, man, cheer up, will you? New Year's, man, supposed to be our grand day out. You're making it like a frigging works outing with Radiohead. Ha'way, we're off for a day out in Whitley Bay, you're into another new flat, we're near our grand total, Toon's fourth in the League, man, I'm telling you, Gerry, things are looking up, man.

They pass smoking, boozing kids.

SEWELL   (CONT.) Hey, and soon we can go back on the good things in life too, cos I tell you, man, I'm bloody desperate now, man. Aye, first thing we do after we've got our tickets: a bit tac man, a bit drink. Go out and get totally peeved. Pure radgie...

GERRY   Sewell..

SEWELL ...Wrecked. Smashed, eh?

GERRY   Sewell man...

SEWELL Mortal, man. Pissed and stoned as farts, eh? *Eh?*

GERRY   Jesus, Sewell man! There *is* no season tickets!

There is a long pause during the entirety of which SEWELL's mouth fails to close. GERRY sighs, and finally opens up.

GERRY   (CONT.) There never will be. My old man found the money... and took it.

Silence. Blood drains from SEWELL's face.

SEWELL All of it?

GERRY   Just after the Sunderland match, he...

SEWELL *Sunderland...?* That was *months* ago, man! And you're just telling us now?

GERRY   You had a canny Christmas, didn't you?

SEWELL Aye?

GERRY   Well, that's why, man. Cos I didn't tell you.

SEWELL *is just too dazed to argue.*

GERRY   (CONT.) Sewell man, I've got the money with me. What we've saved since, like. So if you want to spend it, I'll understand. Have it, man. It's yours. My father's a bastard, that's all there is to it. So take it and be done.

SEWELL stares at him, still pale and stony-faced. But eventually SEWELL's face cracks, the twinkle returns to his eye. It's the only way.

SEWELL   Gerry man... You cannet give up on a mission. Nah, we'll gan down a boozer, us. Hatch a plan, like.

72. INT. BOOZER. WHITLEY BAY SEA FRONT. DAY.

GERRY pays the BARMAN and goes to join RUSTY and SEWELL at a corner table in the smoky pub. SEWELL nods to the television behind the bar. On it we see the opening credits of Crimestoppers.

SEWELL   Ha'way, my favourite programme. It's great. You always see someone you know.

Back to business.

SEWELL   (CONT.) All right, I've worked it out, man. It doesn't seem like we're going to get our tickets *this* season, like, so how's about this? If we can't afford two then maybe we can just get one and share it, like. You one week, me the next. Or I have first halves, you second. Or maybe...

His face freezes as his eye is drawn again to the TV. On it we see CCTV footage that we immediately recognize. GERRY, SEWELL (blind) and RUSTY at the Metro Centre.

TV VOICEOVER   'And have you seen these two teenagers? They work as a team, one about five foot tall, the other over six foot. Here, the taller one poses as a blind person as they steal goods in Gateshead's Metro Centre. They appear to own a dog, white with dark spots. The taller of the two wears a bench-coat of the kind football managers wear.'

The BARMAN, close to the set, racks his brains, positive he's seen these three recently. The light bulb ignites and he turns to see the corner table, empty but for two still-moving pints of beer and some unopened crisps.

73. INT. BRABIN HOUSE. MONCUR ROAD. DAY.

MATTHEW, surrounded by an assortment of scraggy dogs, pulls thoughtfully on a roll-up. MRS BRABIN glances nervously at him but doesn't say a word. MATTHEW clicks Crimestoppers *off with the remote but doesn't take his eye off the screen. He blows smoke out in a long thin pensive jet. His eyes narrow as his memory bank begins to be searched.*

74. EXT. SEA WALL. WHITLEY BAY. DAY.

GERRY is leading the way at a hectic pace along the sea front, looking around with acute paranoia. SEWELL and RUSTY try to keep up. Below them, the waves are breaking against the high sea wall.

GERRY   Shite, man, they may as well have read out our bloody names. Rusty an'all. Even your bloody *bench-coat* got a mention. The whole of Tyneside'll be out looking for us now.

SEWELL   What're we going to do, like?

GERRY comes to a halt.

GERRY   It's pure and simple, Sewell man. I'm sorry... I
           know it'll be hard but... First off, we've got to...
           y'know... Get rid of it.

           *He glances as briefly as he can down at RUSTY.
           RUSTY's return gaze is less fleeting.*

GERRY   (CONT.) You know, I like it as much as you, but
           it's got to go, man. It's a dead giveaway.

SEWELL   Agh, no, man Gerry, I can't do that.

GERRY   It's dangerous, man, you've got to get rid.

SEWELL   I can't do it, man. I've had it for over four years.

GERRY   Eh?

SEWELL   My bench-coat, I've had it four years.

           GERRY looks at him for a moment.

GERRY   Aye, that an'all. But there's something else that's
           got to go.

           *SEWELL looks back at him. The penny finally
           drops.*

SEWELL   Agh... no, man, you can't mean it.

GERRY   Sewell man, that mad Matthew kid'll've seen us.

SEWELL   I can have him easy.

GERRY   He's a radgie, man, a pure psycho.

> *RUSTY jumps up. SEWELL's eyes seem wet.*

SEWELL   Down, boy. I can't do it. I can do my bench-
coat... at a push... but I can't do that. You do it,
man... I can't... You do it... I just can't...

> *He turns his back theatrically and hands over the
> length of twine which is RUSTY's lead.*

GERRY   Don't worry, man, it's all for the best.

SEWELL   I love that dog.

> *RUSTY makes to follow him.*

SEWELL   (CONT.) Stay, Rusty.

> *SEWELL walks sulkily away, head down. GERRY
> looks down at RUSTY, RUSTY looks up at
> GERRY, who promptly shouts after SEWELL:*

GERRY   Sewell man!! *You* should be the one to do this.
It's only right.

> *But SEWELL walks on. GERRY looks further
> along the sea wall, where it bows out high above
> the cold North Sea, a potential spot for the*

dreadful deed. He holds out the noosed rope
towards RUSTY, who approaches uncertainly.
He puts it round the dog's neck. RUSTY is
passive, there is no struggle. CUT TO:

75. EXT. SEA WALL (FURTHER). WHITLEY BAY. DAY.

GERRY picks up the reluctant RUSTY, and
although he talks to him in soft, coaxing tones
(which serve only to alarm RUSTY). He
nevertheless edges him nearer to the top railing.
We see the foaming briny below RUSTY's
perturbed expression.

GERRY   I'm sorry it's got to end this way, Rusty man. But
we can't have people seeing you. You're dead
cute and that, but you're a dead giveaway, man.

He holds him over the drop to the sea.

GERRY   (CONT.) You've been a good dog but, well,
y'know...

76. EXT. SPANISH CITY. WHITLEY BAY. DAY.

Back on the esplanade, GERRY, now dogless,
searches for SEWELL. There are not many
people about, several couples out for a New Year

*walk, but the place – geared towards summer
holiday crowds – feels closed down and sleepy
now. He wanders in to the Spanish City, a
seaside amusement park. As he walks through
the rides, he notices, in the double seat of a
disused Twister-type ride, a figure slumped with
its head on its knees, draped in a big thick coat.
GERRY gives the figure only a cursory glance as
he passes, but then, a few yards on, stops and
slowly returns. Despite the fact that no inch of
flesh is visible, something about the figure is
familiar to him. He gets in and sits next to the
prone body and, for an age, just stares down at
the clump of coat. The shape next to him stirs
slightly. First, hands become visible as the figure
unfolds its arms. Then ears, burrowing out of the
depths of the coat like rabbits from a hole. Hair
follows, then a face. Forehead, cheeks, eyes and
finally mouth. It is who he expected, but a pale
sick shadow of them. He stifles a gasp.*

GERRY   Bridge? What're you doing here?

There is no response.

GERRY   (CONT.) Ha'way man, Bridget, it's me, Gerry.

*We see BRIDGET's face, drawn and exhausted.
A barely recognizable wreck of the young happy
girl we've seen in the photos. She has reached
rock bottom. She fixes her concentration on*

something that seems impossibly distant, screwing up her eyes and replying without looking at him.

BRIDGET All right, Gerry.

With dirty hands she digs out a cigarette and puts it to her mouth as if it was the last one on earth. She drags hard on it, pulling with such concentration it seems like it is taking up all her faculties.

GERRY Where've you been all this time?

Her eyes tell him she's not sure.

GERRY (CONT.) Where've you been sleeping?

BRIDGET Floors mainly... Y'know. Floors... Friends and that... Lived with a lad for a bit. Been all over. Tynemouth, Cullercoats, North Shields. Get caught out sometimes, y'know... Have to spend a night outside now and again. But you just... take something, gets you through... You don't notice the cold then, man.

She smiles a pained smile. GERRY tries to return one but it doesn't arrive. BRIDGET wipes snot from her nose with her sleeve.

GERRY What're you on?

BRIDGET Agh, anything, man Gerry. Tac. E. Wobbly eggs. Speed. Poppers. Smack. Owt. What about you? Still going mental on tac and that?

GERRY No. I've stopped that for a bit, y'know.

BRIDGET leans in closer to GERRY, smiles that sad smile again.

BRIDGET You carrying now?

GERRY I told you, man Bridge, I've...

BRIDGET *(Suddenly aggressive)* Ha'way man Gerry, I know you! Share it with us, man, I'm *desperate*. A bit tac... or owt... Ha'way man I'm your sister!!

GERRY edges away.

BRIDGET (CONT.) You must have something!! Money, you must have *money*. A couple of quid, man Gerry. Ha'way, man, help us out, I'm begging ye, ye fuck.

BRIDGET slumps back down and sinks her head back into her coat. GERRY looks at her, stunned. After a pause, the head comes back out an inch. She is calm once more. GERRY's eyes have welled up.

BRIDGET (CONT.) How's Mam?

GERRY   Not so good, y'know. She's on all these pills
          now, like. Coughing a lot. In the mornings mostly,
          like. And in the afternoon. But... all night mainly.

BRIDGET   Still smoking?

GERRY   Only thing that stops her coughing. She misses
          you, Bridge. We all do. Ha'way, come home,
          won't you?

          BRIDGET is staring at the ground.

GERRY   (CONT.) We've moved again, this time he won't
          find us... It's a canny flat, you should see it. And
          I've sorted your room, with your stuff in it, your
          box and that, put your poster up...

BRIDGET   Gerry, it doesn't matter where it is... it's not home
          any more. This is me life. This. What are you
          doing here anyway?

GERRY   Having a day out, like, with Sewell.

BRIDGET   He still wearing that bench-coat?

GERRY   I bloody hope not. Ha'way, Bridge, come on
          back, eh? Come back and we could do all them
          things we used to do.

BRIDGET   Aye, and so could my dad.

GERRY   I'll look after you.

*BRIDGET reaches a grubby finger to wipe a tear
from GERRY's cheek.*

BRIDGET It wasn't just fists, y'know that, Gerry?... Gerry?

GERRY is looking away, across the funfair.

GERRY   I'm going to kill him. I don't care what they do to
me. They can bang us up for the rest of me life
and hoy away the key and I won't mind, cos it'll
be worth it.

Pause

GERRY   (CONT.) Come on back, Bridge? You don't look
good, y'know?

BRIDGET turns away.

GERRY   (CONT.) H'way, let me tell you where the flat is.

BRIDGET Gerry, I don't want to know.

*Pause. GERRY looks around the fairground, sees
a burger bar.*

GERRY   You want a burger? I'll get you a burger, eh?

BRIDGET *(Forces a smile)* Deep down, Gerry man, you're
still nothing but a bloody angel, you, aren't you?

*He smiles back. She turns away and looks back
down the sea front. GERRY gets up and goes
more chirpily into the burger bar.*

77. EXT. BURGER BAR. SPANISH CITY. WHITLEY BAY. DAY.

*GERRY keeps half an eye on the seat of the
distant ride where BRIDGET sits and half an eye
on the preparation of their burgers. He sees
there is a behind-counter TV on and swiftly pulls
his ski-hat down over his eyes for fear of being
recognized. Another glance at the ride, he sees
BRIDGET lie back down. The burgers are placed
in front of him, he squirts them yellow and red,
pays for them and exits swiftly.*

78. EXT. RIDE. SPANISH CITY. WHITLEY BAY. DAY.

*GERRY arrives back to the ride with the burgers
but the seat is now deserted. Wounded, he looks
quickly round the funfair, but she's gone.*

79. EXT. MEMORIAL. WHITLEY BAY. DAY.

GERRY trudges his dejected way along the promenade eating the burger. He sees SEWELL sitting by the memorial. Surrounded by a carpet of scratched scratch-cards, he is busy scratching another handful. GERRY sits down next to him. It seems like they never parted, like nothing has happened in the last half-hour.

The only noticeable change is that SEWELL's bench-coat is on inside-out. GERRY offers SEWELL BRIDGET's burger, which he hungrily tucks into before sighing in frustration at the last final blank.

GERRY   Where did you get all them?

SEWELL   I nicked them. They're a fucking con.

Pause.

SEWELL   (CONT.) I'm not losing it, Gerry man. I've decided. I'll wear it inside out but that's the limit. Besides, it helps with that other matter. I've been working that out too, and it's sorted. All I've got to do is wear him. Y'know, under my bench-coat, like.

GERRY   What are you on about, man?

SEWELL unzips his bench-coat and RUSTY's head appears. He jumps out in order not to miss out on his share of the burger.

SEWELL   You big soft lad, you. I knew you couldn't do it, man. Tie him to a railing, like? Is that the best you could do?

GERRY   *(Smiles, then)* You can't keep Rusty under your bench coat for ever.

SEWELL   No, I know. Just till Gateshead. Then I'll give him to Gemma to look after for us. Until it's all blown over, like.

GERRY   *Gemma?*

SEWELL   I'm seeing her now, man.

GERRY   You can't be serious.

SEWELL   Why can't I?

GERRY   Because you're... you're you and she's... Engaged, isn't she? To that... frigging Orang-utan Man.

SEWELL   No, no, that's all over, that.

GERRY   Oh aye. Sewell man, the only question now is
who's gonna pull your head out your arse first?
Matthew, the radge dog merchant, or Gemma's
felluh.

SEWELL *I'm* Gemma's felluh.

GERRY   He's an ice-hockey player, man!

SEWELL So?

    *SEWELL crumples up the burger paper into a
ball and stands up.*

GERRY   So? Have you not seen them on telly, man? They
go fucking mental, man. They kill each other over
offside, that lot. And it's not like he'll come after
you on his own. He'll have the whole *squad* with
him, man.

SEWELL Puffs, man. I can have that lot.

    *GERRY shakes his head fondly. SEWELL kicks
the screwed up burger paper.*

SEWELL (CONT.) Shearer! *Shoots!*

    Verbal kid roar.

SEWELL (CONT.) One–nil! Hey, Gerry man. This time next
year, eh? Eh?

GERRY   This time next year, you'll be dead, man. With a
         puck in your gob and a hockey stick up your
         arse.

SEWELL   Shearer! *Two–nil!!*

         *SEWELL gleefully rams home another
         newspaper ball. He notices GERRY is suddenly
         deep in thought.*

SEWELL   (CONT.) What ye thinking, Gerry man?

80. EXT. DUNSTON ROCKET. DAY.

         *FADE UP: This time GERRY is also well wrapped,
         enveloped in a hooded trackie-top. With
         SEWELL in his bench-coat (still on inside-out),
         only tiny amounts of face are visible. GERRY is
         marching at eager pace around the base of the
         Dunston Rocket flats, SEWELL has come to a
         sudden stunned stop. Incredulously:*

SEWELL   You *what?*

GERRY   Keep moving, man, or we'll be recognized.

SEWELL   That's your grand scheme, like? The Great
         Shearer Plan? That's taken you days to work out,
         like? He'll just tell us to fuck off, you know that?

GERRY digs a much-thumbed piece of paper out of his pocket.

GERRY   No, he won't. Look, I've got it all written out. To learn it, like.

SEWELL jogs to catch him up. GERRY begins to read:

'Hallo, Alan, how're you doing? Me and me mate here have been Toon supporters since the day we was born, long before you arrived here from Blackburn. It's...'

SEWELL   You should say 'Mr Shearer'. More formal like. He might go for that. And don't just say 'Blackburn', say 'Blackburn Rovers'. Shows you know your footie, like.

GERRY   '... long before you arrived here from Blackburn Rovers. It's great you came back to Newcastle, the place of your birth.'

SEWELL   Ha'way, he'll have fallen asleep by now.

GERRY   'It's great you came back to Newcastle, the place of your birth.'

SEWELL   You've already told him that once.

GERRY   I'm just finding me place man.

SEWELL   D'you know for sure?

GERRY   What!?

SEWELL   That he was born in Newcastle.

GERRY   Does it matter?

SEWELL   Well, if you're asking a man for season tickets...

GERRY   Sewell, I'll deck you in a minute. 'The
Newcastle... *region*, the place of your birth. My
baby niece is called Sheara.' Personal details,
y'know, make all the difference. 'Unfortunately
we can't get in to see our team, so please give
us a pair of season tickets for the Toon. If you
can't manage two, one'll do like...' Where're you
going? It's this way.

SEWELL has made an unexpected turn.

SEWELL   I said I'd see Gemma before we went.

GERRY   Agh, Jesus.

SEWELL   Ha'way, man, it's hardly out the way.

81. EXT. DUNSTON STAITHES JETTY. DAY

> *GERRY and SEWELL arrive at the jetty, where a huddle of kids are hanging out smoking, swigging a bottle of Lambrusco, dangling from home-made tyre swings etc. Among them are school friends DARREN, MALLY, JIMMY. They are chatting up GEMMA, who has RUSTY on the makeshift lead.*

GEMMA   Areet, lads!

SEWELL   Areet.

DARREN   Areet.

GERRY   Areet.

MALLY   Areet. Hey, you look smaller than you do on telly.

SEWELL   Areet.

GERRY   Areet.

JIMMY   Areet. New bench-coat, Sewell man? About time.

SEWELL   Areet.

GERRY   Areet.

GEMMA   Sewell pet, I've got you your bait, man.

She hands him a snack in a carrier.

GEMMA   (CONT.) It's mostly for you cos I know you'll eat
          the most, being so fat like. But it's for you an'all,
          Gerry man. A few doorsteps and a couple
          o'cans.

SEWELL   Isn't she the best, man? Thanks, pet.

          He gives her a love bite.

MALLY   I don't know, you TV celebs get all the perks.

GEMMA   Is it showing?

          *Proud, he nods and bites her again. The others
          exchange glances. Glances that say that
          SEWELL is not so much out of his depth as
          doomed.*

GEMMA   (CONT.) Ha'way, Sewell, I want a word with you.

          *GEMMA pulls SEWELL further towards the end
          of the jetty, where they kiss again. RUSTY, in
          between them, looks up at them.*

MALLY   They shagging, like?

DARREN   What're you, Inspector fucking Morse?

They look again at SEWELL and GEMMA. They have stopped kissing and SEWELL is looking at her in a most peculiar way.

JIMMY   Where're you going?

GERRY   Nowhere.

MALLY   Is that what Careers Officer said, like?

They laugh. GERRY looks across at SEWELL and GEMMA, who have tied tongues again, seemingly inseparably. MALLY holds out a small bag full of various pills.

MALLY   (CONT.) Here you go, Gerry man. Bag of Lucky Dip.

GERRY shakes his head.

MALLY   (CONT.) H'way, man, a fiver, like.

GERRY   Nah, Sewell and me's off all that.

MALLY   Why, like?

GERRY looks over to the continuing probing of throats.

GERRY   Ha'way, Sewell man, let's get going before you swallow each...

A sudden look of real fear.

GERRY   (CONT.) Oh fuck. Psycho bollocks.

We see, marching along the jetty, the frightening apparition that is MATTHEW BRABIN. Wild, and very scary, even at this distance, a distance that is all too fast receding. He roars at SEWELL.

MATTHEW   Don't ye *move*, man!!

JIMMY, MALLY and DARREN helpfully clear a way as MATTHEW strides past them, then move off in the other direction. They don't want to miss anything, they just want to be spectators at a safer distance. GEMMA too knows danger when she sees it, and immediately and sensibly hands RUSTY's lead over to SEWELL, who stays rooted to the spot as MATTHEW fast approaches. GERRY meanwhile starts taking evasive action with the rest of them, shouting out to SEWELL.

GERRY   Ha'way, Sewell man! He's radgie, off his heed. For God's sake, run, man!

But SEWELL stands his ground. He leans down to pat RUSTY. We see MATTHEW closer. He looks wilder than ever. As he nears SEWELL, he slows down, advancing carefully now that he is so near, like a stalker and, when he gets within

*spitting range of SEWELL, he stops, stares
closely, his bald head leaning to one side like a
dog. SEWELL clears his throat, but his mouth
has run dry.*

MATTHEW   You took my dog. He's mine and you *took* him.

Almost spits this out:

MATTHEW   (CONT.) *Mine!*

SEWELL   I didn't take him, he ...

*Before SEWELL has the chance to finish,
MATTHEW, his eyes growing suddenly and
staggeringly large, launches himself at SEWELL.
With his long fingernails, he grabs SEWELL's
flushed face in his hands and squeezes it hard,
then snarls strangely before opening his mouth
wide, displaying a gleaming tooth-brace, and
clamping his teeth onto SEWELL's nose.
SEWELL, in increasing agony, tries to free his
nose from the vice-like grip of MATTHEW's
molars. Finally, when he seems to be struggling
the most, SEWELL, in a movement flashier and
faster than any we've seen from him throughout
the film so far, brings both hands down on
MATTHEW's neck in a double-whammy karate
chop. MATTHEW's staple-like jaws spring open
and he drops like a sack of spuds to the jetty
floor. SEWELL clutches his nose.*

SEWELL   (CONT.) I didn't take him, he followed me.

> *RUSTY immediately fusses round the barely conscious MATTHEW. SEWELL continues to hold his bleeding nose as he walks off. RUSTY follows. SEWELL barks sternly from underneath his hand:*

SEWELL   (CONT.) *Stay!*

> *Alarmed, RUSTY promptly sits where he is, midway between the departing SEWELL and the horizontal groaning MATTHEW. GERRY falls in with SEWELL as he passes, and together they move through the gawping group of the other three and GEMMA, who part for them. GEMMA has a look of pride on her face. When they are through them and on their own:*

GERRY   What about the hound?

> *SEWELL shakes his head.*

GERRY   (CONT.) You can't leave Rusty, man, you just can't. You love him, you daft get!

> *SEWELL walks on, a faint smile creeping over his bloodied face.*

SEWELL   I've got someone else to love now.

82. INT. BUS TO CHESTER LE STREET. DAY.

> GERRY and SEWELL sit on the bus. GERRY
> gazes out of the window. SEWELL cleans up his
> face with a strange peaceful smile. Out of the
> window GERRY watches the Angel of the North
> go by. It seems to fly as they pass.

GERRY   She's still looking after us, man Sewell, eh?
           What's so funny, like?

SEWELL Eh?

GERRY   What are you smiling at?

SEWELL Ha'way, I'm sorry, man. I'm just happy, man.

GERRY   High more like. What're you on, man?

SEWELL Life, man. Just life.

GERRY   Aye, well, you look frigging gawpy. Give it up, man.
           They'll think we've broken out the funny-farm.

SEWELL Give up smiling?

GERRY   Give up grinning.

SEWELL Can I grin if Shearer gives us our tickets?

GERRY   Not if, Sewell man. When.

83. EXT. MAIN GATE. NEWCASTLE UTD. TRAINING GROUND. DAY.

We see a tight two-shot of SEWELL and GERRY's determined faces. SEWELL whispers:

SEWELL   Ha'way, Gerry man, you don't think all this lot's after season tickets an'all, d'you?

GERRY   No, no one else is that smart, man.

The camera pulls back to reveal that they are only two in a colossal crowd of excited kids. They wait impatiently but silently. Then suddenly the gate opens, and they are like a hundred dogs out of traps. A mass charge towards the Newcastle United players as they emerge, freshly showered.

KIDS   *Alan Alan Alan Alan Alan...!!*

ALAN SHEARER (among other players) stops to grab from the swirling sea of autograph books, pictures and pens. He is pushed and shoved but doesn't complain. He gets through this daily hell with a good-natured smile. The kids continue to shout. GERRY and SEWELL are in among it, but their shouts are lost in the noise.

SEWELL   Hallo Mr Shearer, how're you doing? Me and me mate...!

GERRY   ... Been Toon supporters since the day we was born! Long before you arrived here from Blackburn!

SEWELL   ... Rovers.

> *SHEARER gets nearer and nearer until finally he is so near that SEWELL and GERRY begin not to be able to speak any more. SHEARER is now virtually on top of them. He holds out a hand for a pen and a book, and looks GERRY straight in the eye. It is like the world has stopped still. The sound of the other kids shouting swirls into the background. ALAN SHEARER is looking GERALD MCCARTEN straight in the eye. SHEARER sees the gob-smacked expression and is confused by the lack of anything to sign.*

ALAN SHEARER   What can I do for you, like?

GERRY   Give us a pair of season tickets.

SEWELL   ... one'll do, like, if you can't manage two.

ALAN SHEARER   Oh aye!

> *SHEARER laughs politely, as if hearing a joke for the millionth time. The moment is swamped suddenly by the return of youthful screaming, and with a wry shake of his head SHEARER goes back to pen-pushing work. Within a second, the*

statuesque GERRY and SEWELL are once more at the back of the crowd.

84. EXT. CAR PARK. TRAINING GROUND. DAY.

SEWELL is still in a bit of a daze, but GERRY is now steaming, furious, as livid and as moody as we've seen him so far, as they trudge through a car park full of expensive, flashy, mainly sports cars.

SEWELL   Ha'way, Gerry man, what did you expect?

GERRY   Respect.

SEWELL starts laughing. GERRY's seething.

GERRY   (CONT.) I'll make them take notice of us.

SEWELL   Gerry man, what are you doing?

GERRY is trying car door handles. Eventually one clunks open.

GERRY   Get in.

SEWELL   Gerry man...

GERRY   Just get in, will you?

SEWELL takes a quick glance around and then joins GERRY in the car. GERRY has already ripped off a panel and is hot-wiring the car. The engine roars like a lion.

SEWELL   Gerry, I don't think this is one of your better...

The car screeches out of frame before the word 'ideas' is uttered.

85. INT./EXT. SPORTS CAR. FAST ROAD OUT OF TOWN. DAY.

The sports car roars down the fast lane. We hear GERRY whoop a laugh as he burns the tarmac. He seems too small to be driving. Even in a sports car he looks like a baby at the wheel. SEWELL, on the other hand, seems inordinately big, a roof window would be handy. He also seems strangely concerned, flicking through envelopes in the passenger seat.

GERRY   Ha'way, what a motor, eh? Right fanny-magnet this, eh, Sewell man?

SEWELL   Oh, Jesus, Gerry man.

GERRY   What?

SEWELL   This isn't any old fanny-magnet. It's Alan bloody
         Shearer's fanny-magnet.

GERRY   Eh?

SEWELL   There's all his fan-mail here, look. We're in Alan
         Shearer's bloody motor, man!

         *They stare at each other briefly, in disbelief. Then
         both start to laugh hysterically. We see the car
         roar up the motorway.*

GERRY   Aye, well, that'll teach him to laugh at us.
         Ha'way, Sewell man... He's got a CD player,
         look... Stick one in, man. What's he got?

         *SEWELL looks through a collection of CDs. With
         disapproval.*

SEWELL   Oh, Alan... no, no...

GERRY   What?

SEWELL   It's all the old tarts, man. Des'ree. Natalie
         Imbroolioolio. And that Gabrielle. Y'know, that
         slapper with the patch. Oh, Jesus, no, *Alan!*

GERRY   What?

SEWELL   Celine frigging *Dion!*

86. EXT. WIDE OPEN SPACE. KIELDER. DAY.

*Gabrielle's 'Dreams (Can Come True)' blares out
as the sports car traces a speedy track across
the middle of a panoramic shot of a wide open
nowhere.*

GERRY   ...Well, we're gonna have to wreck it somewhere.

SEWELL   We cannet wreck it man, it's *Shearer's*.

GERRY   Well, we cannet keep driving it either, man. For
         the same friggin' reason. They'll have police
         choppers out soon. We'll have to dump it, like.
         Middle of nowhere somewhere.

SEWELL   What's this then, if it isn't the middle of
         nowhere?

GERRY   Not nowhere enough, that's what.

SEWELL   Great plan, Gerry man. Go to ask Shearer for a
         season ticket and end up twockin his bloody
         motor.

GERRY   Hey but, man, at last, eh? At last.

SEWELL   At last what?

GERRY   Something to tell wor grand-bairns.

87. EXT. FIELD. KIELDER. DAY.

The strains of Gabrielle still blare out from the car speakers as the camera tracks past, in the foreground, Shearer's abandoned sports car, the doors open, parked hurriedly in a field. The skies are black, threatening. Way in the distance we see GERRY and SEWELL running down a hill and away.

88. EXT. HILL TOPS. KIELDER. DAY.

Obviously much later, obviously absolutely knackered, GERRY and SEWELL trudge over fell-tops. They are breathless, exhausted. They come to another brow of another hill and see nothing but more open countryside.

SEWELL   Jesus, it's got to be around here *somewhere*.

GERRY   What?

SEWELL   Newcastle.

The heavens open and in an instant there is torrential rain. They run for shelter.

89. EXT. FOREST. DAY.

GERRY sits on the bank of a deep river, in a deep forest. The rain continues to pour down through the cover of the trees. SEWELL is taking a leak nearby. They are both soaked to the skin. GERRY gazes contemplatively into the black water.

GERRY   Sewell man? Do you ever wonder? Why... you know... we are like we are?

SEWELL   What, drippin' wet and fuckin' lost, like?

GERRY   No, I mean... what decides, like...? You're gonna be brainy, you're not? You're gonna be lucky, you're not? You're gonna have, you're gonna have not?

SEWELL   (O/S) What, like... you're gonna be Keegan, you're gonna be Gullit?

GERRY   Aye. You're gonna be top drawer, like, and you're gonna be scum. Cos that's what we are, you know?

SEWELL   (Proudly) Aye, top drawer.

GERRY   Jesus man, what you *doing*!!

SEWELL is suddenly standing next to GERRY, stripped to his underpants.

SEWELL   If I wanted to listen to a whinin' arsehole, I'd fart, man. H'way, ye gannin for a dip?

SEWELL launches himself into the river like a depth charge. GERRY laughs and goes closer to the bank edge to watch. SEWELL resurfaces, exhilarated.

SEWELL   (CONT.) Belter! It's purely *BELTER!*

The word echoes round the woods. SEWELL laughs, high-pitched with the cold. GERRY laughs with him.

SEWELL   (CONT.) Ha'way, get your kit off, Gerry man, and gerrin!

GERRY thinks for a second, then jolts into action, stripping off his clothes and jumping into the black river too. Even we can feel the cold.

GERRY   It's *freezin'!*

SEWELL   It's *cushdy!*

GERRY   It's bloody *freezin'!!*

He's plainly telling the truth. He swims round in small hurried circles. Through chattering teeth:

GERRY   (CONT.) C-canny spot to b-bring a lass, this, man, eh? Make sure she d-doesn't bring a c-cozzie, eh? Get a few handfuls in under the water, like. Then after, t-take her under that tree there, warm her up, like, rub her down, smooth away any of them g-goose-bumps, y'know. Then chat her up like, tell her stories... Like the day you t-t-twocked Shearer's motor... T-telling you, open any lass's legs, that one. Then lay pipe like there's no tomorrow. What you think, eh? Sewell? Sewell man, I'm talking to you!

But SEWELL is standing still, the water round his waist. He is as still as a statue, gazing down into the river close to him. He very slowly lowers a hand into the water.

SEWELL   Stay still, Gerry man, don't you move.

GERRY stops swimming for a second and nearly sinks. With a sudden but enormous movement, SEWELL flings his arm into the air. Water fills the sky. A large flapping fish flies through it and thuds onto the river bank.

SEWELL   (CONT.) Our tea.

He smiles at GERRY, for whom it takes a seriously stunned second to smile back. CUT TO:

90. EXT. FOREST. NIGHT.

GERRY and SEWELL are gold-lit by a crackling fire they have made. On the fire a hubcap plays pan to the sizzling fish. They take it in turns to aimlessly prod it with sticks.

SEWELL   I could eat a scabby donkey, me.

GERRY   Aye, and all we've got's a scabby fish. Where did you learn that then? Fishing with your mits, like?

SEWELL   My dad learned us. When I was a bairn, like.

GERRY   Did he learn you lots of stuff like that? Your old man?

SEWELL   My dad's not me old man.

GERRY frowns.

SEWELL   (CONT.) I live with my grandad, I just *call* him my dad. I never knew my dad. Or my mam.

GERRY   What happened to them?

SEWELL   Nowt. They just went off, like. I was just... something they didn't need.

GERRY   Do you not, you know... want to find them?

SEWELL   I'd only kill 'em.

GERRY   *(Clearly identifies with the scenario)* Maybe that's
what I was on about... You know, what makes
you what y'are. Maybe that's it – A good dad.
One that loves you..., wants you and that.

SEWELL   Aye. A good dad. That's what I'm gonna be.

GERRY   Aye, me too.

SEWELL   No... I mean soon, Gerry man. I'm gonna be a
father. Gemma's... you know...

*GERRY and SEWELL look at each other. A long
silent beat.*

GERRY   You sure it's yours, like?

SEWELL   Fuck off, Gerry man, Gemma's a lady.

GERRY   Gemma's Gemma, Sewell man. And she's
fourteen.

SEWELL   So? We'll have longer together.

Another silent pause.

GERRY   You could always... you know... I mean it's not
too late to...

SEWELL   Gerry man, I'm happy about it, right? Dead
          happy. Happier than I've ever been about
          anything. In my whole life. Right?

          GERRY, stung, stares into the fire. We hear the
          strike of a match and see SEWELL lighting up
          possibly the fattest joint in the history of Tyne
          and Wear.

GERRY   Jesus man, what's that!?

SEWELL   Silk Cut.

GERRY   We've stopped all that man! We gave it all up for
          our season tickets.

SEWELL   No team's that good, man.

          GERRY looks angry. SEWELL pulls on the joint,
          holds it, then emits a cloud of smoke which he
          wallows in.

SEWELL   (CONT.) Gerry man. The season ticket thing...
          That was just about... having a bit of fun, wasn't
          it? Something to do, like.

GERRY   Was?

SEWELL   It was great, but it was just a game, wasn't it?
          Just... dreaming of better things, like. Of being
          something.

GERRY knows what's coming.

SEWELL (CONT.) I don't have to dream no more.

> *He hands the joint over to GERRY, who looks at it for a long time before, with a tinge of sad resignation, he takes it. A beat. GERRY pulls hard on the joint. It's been a long time. FADE TO BLACK.*

91. INT. SUPERMARKET. DAY.

> *The screen is chock-a-block with blocks o'chock. A huge supermarket dump of large, gaudy Easter eggs with bows and hearts fill the screen with a pattern of garish colours. A title:*

'Spring'

> *Suddenly the dump collapses. The egg-boxes cascade to the floor and, as staff hurry around to begin the task of rebuilding we see, among the mayhem, SEWELL walking away, surreptitiously slipping the culprit egg into the dark recesses of his bench-coat.*

92. INT. ASTORIA BINGO HALL. DAY.

A once grand Cinema Theatre is now a run-down but well-attended Bingo Hall. Among the crowd, CLARE (with SHEARA), MAM and GERRY sit in a line, each flicking off numbers as the CALLER announces them through a bass-heavy microphone on stage where a screen also displays the number. On the backdrop a sign reads Cash Prize £500. GERRY looks like he is about to burst.

MAM   Gerry, son, ye areet?

GERRY   I only need one... I only need number eight.

MAM   Jesus...

GERRY starts muttering to himself.

GERRY   Eight, c'mon, eight, eight, eight. This is it, man...

He loses all control of his body, which rises involuntarily.

Close-up of CALLER.

CALLER   ... Alan Shearer, number nine. We cut to the screen which reads: Nine.

DISTANT PLAYER   *(Loud) House!!*

GERRY   (Even louder) Fuck! Agh fuck fuck FUCK!

MAM   It's the University o'Life, Gerry son. You just
             graduated.

             *She laughs sympathetically. But the laugh turns
             swiftly into a coughing fit. Not so much a fit as a
             full-blooded attack. The veins in her throat bulge
             and her purple face strains for air. The camera
             moves in on GERRY's stunned face. From
             season ticket to seriously sick mother in five
             seconds. CUT TO:*

93. INT. HOSPITAL WARD. DAY.

             *MAM lies in a bed in a crowded hospital ward.
             She looks thin and drawn. Tubes lead in and out
             of her arms. Her hair is damp against her
             forehead. An oxygen mask lies close at hand.
             GERRY holds tightly onto her hand.*

MAM   I think I'm sick this time, pet.

GERRY   The doctor says you'll be all right.

MAM   What does he know? He's only eleven. No... I
             think... I'm knackered, son.

             *MAM takes her hand from GERRY's in order to
             place the mask over her mouth. Her eyes close*

with relief. *GERRY stares at her for a sad second. She then removes the mask briefly, her eyes still closed.*

MAM   (CONT.) Let me rest now, Gerry pet, I'm tired...

She drifts off. A long pause now as GERRY stares at the state of his mother. The sadness in his eyes is replaced by a look of growing anger, which slowly builds until, with a scrape of his chair, he jumps up and runs out of the ward.

94. INT. CORNER CAFF. DAY.

A colossal Easter egg rests on a café table. In front of it another male hand rests on another female one. The camera pulls back to reveal a beaming SEWELL sitting opposite GEMMA.

GEMMA   Hell, it's massive, man Sewell.

SEWELL Aye, but you're scoffing for two now, like.

He smiles. She doesn't. She looks down at her hand and, another parting of hands, removes it slowly from under SEWELL'S, which remains there, empty, on the table. He looks at her but she looks anywhere but back. SEWELL's not that bright, but he's not that dim either. He looks like a seal about to be culled.

SEWELL   (CONT.) Gemma...?

GEMMA   I'm just gone fifteen, Sewell man, I cannet handle
all that stuff.

She feels his stare burn into her, faces him.

GEMMA   (CONT.) I had to do it, Sewell, I had no choice... If
he found out... that'd be it, like.

SEWELL   Who...?

It dawns.

SEWELL   (CONT.) Zak? You're still with...?

GEMMA   Sewell man, you're a dead nice lad and that. And
I love you loads, man, it's just... Zak's got a job,
like. A future, y'know? And you've got...

*She trails off before she says 'nothing', but the
insinuation is clear.*

SEWELL   Not now I haven't.

95. EXT. HIGH BRIDGE. RIVER TYNE. DAY.

*GERRY sprints as fast as he can along the
walkway of the high bridge above the Tyne. He is
crying. Breathless.*

96. INT. CORNER CAFF. DAY.

SEWELL's eyes have welled up too. And, like GERRY's before, they also contain an increasing anger.

GEMMA   It's just... I've got a chance, y'know? A real chance, like... to have a... decent life. You can understand that, can't you, Sewell man? Sewell?

He can't. To go with the sorrow, anger and now confusion, a hint of madness also appears in SEWELL's eyes. He stands suddenly, abruptly, and, on his quick exit, punches the Easter egg with sheer rage.

97. EXT. PUBS (NEAR THE CENTRE). NEWCASTLE. DAY.

We see GERRY run quickly into and quickly out of three different pubs. His anger is mounting.

98. INT. ICE RINK. LEISURE CENTRE. DAY.

The mad look still in his eye, SEWELL opens the gate onto the ice rink where the Sunderland Chiefs are practising.

SEWELL   You! *You, you bastard!!*

He marches, slips, falls, runs, skids, tumbles, as
he aims for the masked giant with, 'Frezackerley'
on his back. It is a ludicrous situation, a guy in a
bench-coat, trackies and trainers slip-sliding like
Bambi to take on a mammoth, massively padded
ice-hockey goalie. By the time he reaches him
SEWELL has finally got up some speed, a fair
proportion of it unintentional. He thumps into
ZAK, pushing him into the goal. Any semblance
of a game immediately stops, but the skating
accelerates, as players from both teams rush to
help their colleague. GERRY was right, they are
as mental as they are on the telly.

99. INT. WORKING MEN'S CLUB. DAY.

GERRY skids breathlessly into the sparsely
populated WMC, where a boozy lunchtime
gaggle pay absolutely no attention to the on-
stage Karaoke entertainment supplied by DAD.
GERRY stops a moment, watching as a tick-
tacky backing track goes too fast for his DAD,
who, in a cloud of cigarette smoke and Newcy
Brown fumes, murders Presley with alcoholic
poisoning. GERRY approaches his DAD. His
DAD, closing one eye to focus, sees him coming.

DAD
'Maybe I didn't treat you
Quite as good as I could have
Maybe I didn't love you
Quite as often as I should have
Little things I should have said and done
I just never took the time
You were always on my mind
You were always on my mind.'

GERRY   Mam's sick.

DAD   Eh? *'Maybe I didn't hold you...'*

GERRY   She's in hospital.

DAD   *'... All those lonely lonely nights...'* Do I look like someone who gives a fuck?

GERRY   You should do, you put her there.

DAD   *'And I guess I never told you...*
I'm so happy that you're mine...'

GERRY   Dad...?

DAD   *'If I made you feel second best...'* Agh, just fuck off son, eh? *'I'm so sorry I was blind...'*

The camera closes in on GERRY as his shoulders finally drop. He turns and slowly walks out of the pub.

DAD   'You were always on my mind...
               You were always on my mind...'

               FADE TO BLACK.

100. EXT. ANGEL OF THE NORTH. DAY.

*FADE UP: GERRY sits alone, head down, at the
base of the Angel. It looks like some time has
passed. Some pretty bad time. He looks drawn,
sick. In his hands is a small plastic bag. He pulls
it slowly up to his face, covering his nose and
mouth. Before he inhales, a figure appears
suddenly beside him. It's SEWELL. He has a
battered, pummelled scab-scarred face.*

GERRY   Fuck, Sewell man... what happened...?

               Sewell speaks with difficulty:

SEWELL   You should see the state of *them.*

               He indicates plastic bag.

SEWELL   (CONT.) What you doing, Gerry man?

GERRY   I'm like you, man... Still waiting for them better
               things.

SEWELL shakes his head sadly, then looks up at the Angel. He booms:

SEWELL   *I hope you're right proud of yourself, you!! You big fucking twat! You were meant to see us through, man!*

GERRY watches SEWELL wince from such mouth-movement, then looks back up to the Angel.

GERRY   What made you come here, Sewell man?

SEWELL   I don't know, I just...

Sees GERRY looking up at the Angel, then slowly looks up at it again himself. Then they look at each other. Battered kids, with a sudden fresh glint in their eyes.

101. EXT. MONUMENT. TUBE STATION. DAY.

SEWELL and GERRY rise on the escalator in the underground station. They look possessed, both have a mad but determined look in their eyes. GERRY's arms are pumping like pistons. SEWELL, despite the fresh limp, keeps up with him. They walk faster than they have walked so far.

SEWELL   Eh?

GERRY   It's the only way, man. The whole lot in one job.
         One big job, we're there. Are you with me, man
         Sewell?

SEWELL   I'm with you, Gerry man. When though?

GERRY   Today.

SEWELL   *Today?*

GERRY   Now.

SEWELL   *Now?*

         *They gather pace in the tube station concourse
         and climb the steps into Grey Street above.*

SEWELL   (CONT.) Where?

GERRY   I don't know. Wherever we are when we finish
         the song.

SEWELL   *Eh?*

101A EXT. GREY STREET. DAY.

         GERRY breaks into a jog. SEWELL follows suit.

GERRY   No turning back, right?

SEWELL   No turning back.

            They break into a trot, and eventually into quiet,
            muttered song.

GERRY   It'll be great man, we'll go to every match. Sitting
            in our own seats. Shut your eyes man. *'Ah me*
            lads... ye shoulda seen us gannin...'

SEWELL   *(Closes his eyes as he runs too)* Aye. Drinking
            our own tea. Two sugars, *dead* milky man.
            '...Passin the folks along the road
            Just as they were stannin'.'

GERRY   And nobody to tell us what to do.

SEWELL   Belter.

GERRY   Purely belter.

            They break into a sprint now as they run past a
            long row of shops, take-aways, bookies, mini-
            marts, etc.

GERRY AND SEWELL   *'Aal the lads an lasses there*
            aal wi smilin faces...
            Gannin alang the Scotswood Roooooooad
            T'see the... Blaydon Races.'

They skid to a halt and open their eyes to look up at the target of their 'big job'. A simultaneous look of huge uncertainty takes over their faces.

SEWELL Fuck, Gerry man, are you sure?

We cut to a wide shot revealing them to be outside the open door of an enormously grand bank.

GERRY No turning back.

SEWELL *(Very worried)* Aye but... what's the plan, like?

GERRY There isn't one. Take your jacket off.

They take off their jackets and roll them around their arms. Then they pull their ski-hats down over their faces and enter the bank as confident as any desperate, clueless, planless, amateur, adolescent bank robbers could be.

102. INT. BANK. DAY.

It's a colossal branch. There are many cashiers at a central service area. A MALE CUSTOMER is being served at one, an ELDERLY FEMALE one at another. Elsewhere, a grey-suited BUSINESSMAN is at the Enquiries window. A WOMAN is just leaving as GERRY and SEWELL march dramatically, determinedly in, hats over faces, coats round arms.

MAUD   Ha'way! All right, Gerry son? All right, Sewell?

GERRY and SEWELL freeze. After a sweaty beat:

GERRY   All right, Auntie Maud...

SEWELL   Mrs Jackson.

MAUD   Eeh, what are you two playing at? You look like you're robbing the bank!

She laughs a smoker's laugh. GERRY reluctantly lifts his hat a few inches up his face.

GERRY   ...No... just... cold, like...

MAUD   How's your mam? I hear she's had a turn, like.

GERRY   She's... all right, like. Em... I can't stop, Auntie Maud, we're in a rush, like.

MAUD   Oh aye, no rest for the wicked, eh? See you.

With that, she's gone. GERRY and SEWELL look around the bank, look at each other, clueless. SEWELL throws a 'what now?' expression. GERRY gestures for him to stay where he is, then pulls his hat down over his face again, and

stands in the queue behind the MAN. There is a
nervous, seemingly eternal lack of action.
SEWELL looks ridiculous, hat over head,
stranded in the wide open space of the floor with
nothing to do but stand there looking ridiculous.
The MAN in the queue finishes and leaves,
revealing the waiting, urgent GERRY, but the
CASHIER doesn't even look up, placing her
'Desk Closed' sign in her window.

CASHIER 1   Next window please.

The ski-hat looks stunned. Its voice is muffled to
incomprehension:

GERRY   Mut ah'm rommin nuh mank.

CASHIER 1   *(Still not looking up)* Sorry?

GERRY   Ah'm rommin nuh mank.

CASHIER 1   Next window please.

The CASHIER still doesn't look up and the hat
still looks stunned. It turns around to look at
SEWELL. Then the OLD LADY leaves the next
window and GERRY jumps straight to it.

GERRY   Giffa fouffum moum!

The male CASHIER smiles, ducks his head in an attempt to see the face.

CASHIER 2   I'm sorry?

GERRY finally accepts that hat disguise and communication don't mix, and lifts the hat above his mouth.

GERRY   Gissa thousand pounds.

For the first time, the CASHIER is slightly suspicious that this is not after all University Rag Week.

CASHIER 2   Um, have you got an account number?

GERRY   No, but I've got a fucking gun.

The CASHIER smiles again, but with a hint of nervousness now.

CASHIER 2   Come on now, lad, a joke's a...

GERRY jumps a pace back and dramatically brings his hands up to the window, pointing his rolled coat directly at the cashier.

GERRY   This isn't a fucking joke, man! I'm serious! Laugh arrus again, I'll blow yer bloody head off! Now give us a thousand pounds!

All other bank staff dive to the floor. The
BUSINESSMAN at Enquiries is stranded, but
SEWELL jumps into action at last, taking a
similar gun-pointing pose, pushing his rolled
coat to the man's chest.

SEWELL   Give him the money or this felluh gets it!!

Even below the hat, we can tell GERRY is
thinking SEWELL watches too much television.
Behind the counter, CASHIER 2 prods a floor
button with his toe.

CASHIER 2   All right, all right, calm down. Just a
thousand?

GERRY   What?

CASHIER 2   You only want a thousand?

GERRY   Em... Yeah...

CASHIER 2   How do you want it...?

GERRY   How do I want it...? I d'know... Quickly?

The CASHIER reaches for the drawer.

CASHIER 2   I only have three hundred in my drawer. I have
to go to the back there to get the rest.

GERRY   All right, but don't you go pressing no buttons!

Over in the far corner, the BUSINESSMAN
speaks quietly:

BUSINESSMAN   That's just a coat. You haven't *got* a gun.

Horrible nervous pause.

SEWELL   You can't be sure.

BUSINESSMAN   Pretty sure. There's nothing in there.

Horrible pause two. The CASHIER is unlocking
another drawer.

GERRY   *(Distant)* C'mon c'mon...

SEWELL   Not a hundred per cent sure, though, are you?

BUSINESSMAN   Ninety-nine.

Horrible pause three. The CASHIER pulls out a
wad of notes.

SEWELL   Take a walk, then, if you feel lucky. Eh? Do you
feel lucky, punk?

BUSINESSMAN   Actually, I do quite.

SEWELL   Em... Gerry, man...!?

GERRY Agh, Jesus... don't use wor fuckin *names*, Sewell man... Agh, shite.

Suddenly, the have-a-go hero BUSINESSMAN has grabbed SEWELL's plainly empty rolled bench-coat. SEWELL tries to pull it back, then decides to pull up his ski-hat to reveal his recently bashed face. It is a bloody terrifying sight.

BUSINESSMAN Good God...

With that, SEWELL head-butts him. Unfortunately it gives SEWELL much much *more grief than it does the BUSINESSMAN, re-opening one of his hockey-stick wounds. He staggers blindly around the bank, grasping his bleeding nose.*

SEWELL Agh, fuck fuck, Jesus...

GERRY can see the thousand pounds approaching the counter.

GERRY Give it here man, give it here. What's...?

We hear approaching police sirens.

GERRY (CONT.) Agh you fucker, man! *Give it here! Give it man!*

The CASHIER pushes the money very slowly towards the window. The nearer it gets, the louder the sirens. Finally, GERRY has a hold of it, but the CASHIER fails to let go. A tug-of-war starts...

SEWELL   Ha'way, Gerry man... I mean... Kevin man... Let's get out! Leave it, man...!

...and ends with a short sharp rip. The result, Barclays Bank, £995, Gerry £5. Or half a £5, it being ripped down the middle. He shakes his head in bewilderment, almost offended – 'How could you do this?' There is a screech of brakes outside.

GERRY   It was only for our tickets, man, that's all!

ARMED POLICE crash in through the doors. We hear the thunk of a police cell door.

103. INT. POLICE CELL. NIGHT.

GERRY and SEWELL, sitting alongside each other on a bench in the police cell, look, despite the exhaustion and the battle-scars, ridiculously young and innocent. GERRY holds up the torn fiver.

GERRY   A year nearly. Nearly a fucking year. And this is
           all we've got.

SEWELL   We going to split it? 50-50, like?

GERRY   It's not funny, Sewell man.

SEWELL   We can give it to me dad when he visits. He can
           bury it somewhere. He'll never remember where
           he buried it, mind.

GERRY   Sewell man...

SEWELL   But if he did, we could escape and fly to Spain.
           Ey, splash out on a couple o'season passes at
           Real Madrid.

           A POLICEMAN enters with two polystyrene cups.

POLICEMAN   Two teas.

           SEWELL looks into the tea, concerned.

SEWELL   Can I have it more milky?

           *Before the POLICEMAN completes his stare of
           utter contempt, a second POLICEMAN enters.*

POLICEMAN 2   Which of you's McCarten?

           GERRY looks up.

POLICEMAN 2   (CONT.) The hospital's been on... There's some... bad news, like.

Close-up of GERRY – how much worse can things get?

104. INT. CREMATORIUM. DAY.

In the chapel, the camera tracks past a coffin and on to the VICAR, who is in the process of spewing the routine pseudo-grief of which all vicars are so capable.

VICAR   And so we say a final goodbye to a much-loved and fondly cherished member of our community...

The camera tracks past a sleeping SHEARA, held by a tearful CLARE, comforted by a strangely dispassionate GERRY, and finally settles on a very serene, and slightly fitter-looking MAM.

VICAR   (CONT.) ...A loving husband, a doting father, a loyal friend, cruelly taken from us during a moment's lack of concentration crossing the inner ring road late last Thursday night. We will all miss... Billy McCarten...

GERRY   Thank fuck the bus-driver didn't.

> The VICAR is momentarily phased, but
> nevertheless invites them to:

VICAR   Please, now, all stand for the hymn, 'Now Thank
         We All Our God.'

> FADE TO BLACK.

105. INT. JUVENILE COURT. DAY.

> Not a grand courtroom, more of a big office. We
> see GERRY standing behind a table in a cheap
> suit, white shirt and sober tie. The camera pulls
> back to show SEWELL alongside him, flannel
> trousers, white shirt, sober tie and bench-coat.
> Sitting at the table also are a LAWYER and
> MAUREEN. Behind them, among others, are
> CLARE, SHEARA, MAM and MR SEWELL. They
> are all listening to a droning MAGISTRATE:

BEAK   Despite having heard very positive accounts
         regarding the character of these two... youths...
         it would be remiss to ignore the gravity of this
         particular... misdemeanour.

> SEWELL spots something out of the window,
> smiles with a certain amount of pride, and
> nudges GERRY to look. GERRY smiles too, and
> leans to whisper to SEWELL:

GERRY   Your spelling's coming on, man.

We see what they see: outside in the council gardens, a flower-bed we recognize, full of daffodils that spell the word:

BOLLUCKS

They are both smirking as the summing-up continues:

BEAK   However, the evidence heard plainly indicates that this was hardly the work of hardened criminals. Indeed the fact that the accused put a ceiling limit on their cash demands leads one to suspect that this was quite clearly a first-time effort. In the hope that it will also be a *last* time, I sentence Gerald McCarten and James Sewell each to two hundred hours' community service over the next twelve months.

Books and files are closed, chairs scrape, doors open. GERRY and SEWELL look slightly shaken. MAUREEN pats them both on the shoulders.

GERRY   Two hundred?

MAUREEN   It'll fly by.

GERRY and SEWELL are seriously unconvinced.

FADE TO BLACK.

106. INT. BLEAK CORRIDOR. DAY.

FADE UP: GERRY and SEWELL, wearing Newcastle shirts to work in, wheel a trolley full of small foil containers along a corridor full of doors. They are faintly whistling 'Blaydon Races'. We rapidly intercut between door buzzers, doorbells, doors being answered by various OLD PEOPLE, referred to by surnames only, their various tables being set, and their various thanks being said. Also intercut is the close-up preparation of two mugs of milky tea. The meals-on-wheels are carried out in a very businesslike manner, but quite hurried and not particularly over-friendly. Until:

107. INT. MRS HARVEY'S FLAT. DAY.

The door opens and the elderly and infirm MRS HARVEY beams with delight.

MRS HARVEY   Hiya, me lads, how are *you* twos?

GERRY   Areet, Beryl, you?

SEWELL   Areet, Beryl pet?

MRS HARVEY   Aye, all the better for seeing you, like.
Come in, come in.

*GERRY and SEWELL quickly, kindly and
efficiently lay her table, help her sit down at it,
open up her food, serve it out for her.*

MRS HARVEY   Thanks, me little angels. Ey, nearly time,
lads. Your tea's on the side there. I'll see you
later, eh?

*GERRY and SEWELL grab their mugs of dead
milky tea, then wander through her flat to the
balcony window, which they slide open.*

108. EXT. BALCONY. MRS HARVEY'S FLAT. DAY.

*On the balcony are two battered but comfy-
looking old armchairs. GERRY and SEWELL step
out and sink snugly into them. We see their faces
immediately glow with a look of extraordinary
well-being, the state of pure contentment that is
known in local parlance as...*

GERRY   Cushdy. Eh?

SEWELL   Aye. Cushdy.

109. EXT. BALCONY FROM DISTANCE. DAY.

We see GERRY and SEWELL sipping their tea with relish. As the camera pans round to take in their viewpoint, we hear a huge roar, and then we see it. Packed and noisy, the place erupting in a mass of noise, music, balloons and tickertape, we see Newcastle United run out onto the enormous St James's Park below. It's a bird's-eye view but, bloody hell, who's complaining?

END